The Harwich
Naval Forces

The Harwich
Naval Forces

Their Part in the Great War
1914–1918

E. F. Knight

LEONAUR

The Harwich Naval Forces: Their Part in the Great War, 1914-1918
by E. F. Knight

Leonaur is an imprint of Oakpast Ltd

Material original to this edition and presentation of the
text in this form copyright © 2011 Oakpast Ltd

ISBN: 978-0-85706-627-5 (hardcover)
ISBN: 978-0-85706-628-2 (softcover)

http://www.leonaur.com

Publisher's Notes

The views expressed in this book are not necessarily
those of the publisher.

Contents

Preface

Recent visits that were made to Harwich for the purpose of writing a series of articles on the Harwich Naval Forces for the *Morning Post* suggested to me the amplification of these articles and their reproduction in the form of a little book. This does not profess to be anything more than a summary of the gallant doings of the Harwich Forces in the course of the war. The full history, no doubt, will be written some day. But this, I hope, may serve as a record that will enable many to realise better what Britain owes to the navy, and what a great work was done by the light cruisers, destroyers, submarines, and auxiliary vessels that had Harwich as their base throughout the war.

For the purposes of this book I have referred to no official records. Conversations with those who were eye-witnesses of and participators in the events that I have here described have served as my sole source of information.

My thanks are due to the naval officers who so readily assisted me in my quest while I was in Harwich, and to the *Morning Post* for the kind permission which I have received to publish in book form my articles that appeared in that paper.

E. F. K.

PART 1

The Harwich Force

Chapter 1

The Opening of the War

He who undertakes to write the history of the Naval Forces which had Harwich as their base during the Great War will have a wonderful story indeed to tell—from the sinking, within a few days of the declaration of war, of the German mine-layer *Königin Luise* by a section of the force, down to the day when there steamed into Harwich harbour, under the escort of the Harwich Force, the surrendered submarines of the beaten enemy. To those who manned our ships during those four terrible years it must all seem now like some strange dream—the weary, watchful patrolling through storm or fog, with no lights showing on sea or shore; the feeling of the way by dead reckoning and lead in dark wintry weather along the enemy's coasts, with an ever-vigilant foe above, below, and on the surface of the sea; the amazing adventures; the risks boldly taken; and ever and anon an action fought with a fierce determination on both sides.

For the Germans fought bravely and skilfully on occasion during the first years of the war. One gathers that it was not until the end that their morale began to weaken. They thought that they could shake the morale of the British Navy by methods of frightfulness, by the cold-blooded murder of the survivors of sinking ships, and so forth. But it was their own morale that failed at last. For this parvenu German Navy, good though its ships and good its personnel, was lacking in one essential—the tradition that inspires our own navy, the significance of which tradition the German, who knows not chivalry, is incapable of understanding. A navy with an old and glorious tradition could not have surrendered itself, as did the German Navy, without having come out and made a fight—if hopeless fight—of it, as did the Spanish ships off Cuba and the Russians at Chemulpo, so saving the honour of their flag.

It is part of the tradition, too, of the British Navy at all cost to stand by a friend in distress. It will be remembered that at the beginning of the war two important ships were torpedoed while rescuing the crews of sinking consorts, and that this led to the issue of an admiralty order to the effect that no heavy ships must risk valuable material by undertaking this dangerous work, which should be left to the light craft. The zeal that comes of an old tradition may need checking at times, but it leads to victory in the end. Had the *Blücher* belonged to a navy with a tradition, it is improbable that she would have been deserted, as she was, by the Germans after her disablement.

To any Englishman who, in these days of the armistice, looks across Harwich harbour and the broad estuary of the Stour, that scene, composed of grey wintry sky, grey sea, and grey warships at anchor, will remain to him as a stirring memory. For those are the light cruisers and destroyers of the Harwich Force, and there, too, is the Submarine Flotilla—all these have fought in the Great War; some throughout the war; while others have joined the force later to replace ships that have been lost in action. On board these ships are still the crews that fought them. No doubt shortly ships and men will be dispersed. But at present they remain here in readiness, for it is not Peace yet. Higher up the Stour, a token of victory, lie the surrendered German submarines, on account of their dirty condition more plainly visible through the haze than are our own ships; for the Huns, naturally, before giving them up, wasted no paint on the outside of these craft, and certainly no soap within.

What is known as the Harwich Force, towards the end of 1914, was composed of the light cruisers *Arethusa*, *Fearless*, *Undaunted*, and *Aurora*, and forty destroyers forming two flotillas. The force gradually increased its strength of light cruisers, being joined at various times by the *Penelope*, *Conquest*, *Cleopatra*, *Canterbury*, *Carysfoot*, and others. Commodore Tyrwhitt—now

Rear-Admiral Sir Reginald Tyrwhitt—commanded the force from the beginning, his first flagship being the *Arethusa*. He is still in command of the force, with the *Curaçoa* as his flagship.

Various were the duties performed by this light force—the patrolling of the enemy's coasts, keeping the Grand Fleet informed of the enemy's movements, the perpetual harassing of the enemy, the hunting down of his submarines and mine-layers, the enticing out of his heavy ships to fall into our traps, the convoying of merchantmen, and so forth. The work was extremely important and highly dangerous. Throughout the war there was always some portion of the Harwich Force upon the seas, and always a portion of it in harbour under steam, ready to rush out at a moment's notice should the wireless waves give notice of something doing on the North Sea. On one occasion practically the entire Harwich Force got out of harbour within twenty minutes of a call for its assistance. Even when there was no urgency, no longer than three hours' notice was ever given.

A force so actively engaged as was this one could not fail to suffer many casualties—in all probability heavier casualties in proportion to its numbers than any other naval force. Admiral Lord Jellicoe, on one occasion, in a message of greeting to the force, said: "Your casualties alone in this war show what your work has been," or words to that effect. What the total casualties of the force were I do not know; but the narratives that have been communicated to me account for the total loss of over twelve of the destroyers, while the number of others seriously damaged by shell, mines, and torpedoes is still larger.

Harwich, possibly, was nearer to the war and its tragedies than any other port in England. For often, by day or in the quiet night, would be heard the weird signal of the sirens that summoned officers and men on leave on shore to hurry back to their ships, as something was happening on the North Sea that called for the Harwich Force, or a portion of it, to put to sea at once. This recall signal, say those who heard it in Harwich, had a most impressive effect. Taking the time from the flagship, each cruiser in the harbour sounded both her sirens three times, each blast being of three minutes' duration.

There is an hotel overlooking the water at Dovercourt—one of the few that had not been requisitioned by the authorities—that was a well-known rendezvous of officers during the war. Situated about half way between Harwich pier and Parkeston quay—whither men had to go to join their ships—and about a quarter of an hour's walk from either place, it was recognised as being a convenient place of call for naval officers who were on shore for a few hours in those days of sudden summons. It had been arranged, too, that the hotel telephone should always supplement the message of the siren. At this hotel—and, by the way, what a scene was here when the armistice was announced!—there were always staying numbers of the relatives and friends of the naval officers. There was often a gay assemblage here. It was the gaiety of brave men at the prospect of danger, and of women who concealed their anxiety for the sake of their men. On one occasion, when the loud siren's call, dreaded of women, came, a concert for the benefit of some naval or military fund was just opening in the great hall belonging to the hotel, and the wives and other ladies related to the naval officers were selling the programmes. There was no time for farewells; the officers left the hall and hurried down the unlit, narrow streets of the old town to the quays as fast as they were able. But the concert was not interrupted, and, assuming a brave face, the ladies continued to sell the programmes. As on other occasions, of the men who left the hall that night there were some who did not come back.

There are many who were in Harwich during the war who can now read Byron's stanzas describing the scene at Brussels on the eve of Waterloo with an understanding mind. This war has shown that the spirit of the Elizabethan and Nelson days is still with us. One wonders how the people of ages hence, when, from a long way off, they look back at these "*old, unhappy, far-off things and battles long ago*," will think and write of the men and women of this day.

The Harwich Force lost no time in going out to search for the enemy after the declaration of war. War was declared by Great Britain on August 4, 1914, and at an early hour of the morning following that fateful event the people of Harwich thronged the quays and the seashore to witness the steaming out of the harbour at high speed of the entire Harwich Force. It was a scene of wild enthusiasm on shore, and the population loudly cheered the ships that were hurrying off to fight the enemies of England.

It was at six in the morning of that glorious summer day that the force left the harbour, and then the ships spread out in accordance with orders. At 9 a.m. a section of the force, consisting of the light cruiser *Amphion* and some destroyers, were near the Galloper, when Captain Fox, commanding the *Amphion*, hoisted the cheery signal, "*Good hunting!*" It was a signal that typified the sporting spirit in which our navy went to work from the beginning to the end of the war. Soon the chance came to this flotilla of firing the first shots that were fired in the naval war.

At 10.30 the *Königin Luise*, a German mail steamer that had been fitted out as a mine-layer, was sighted. Chased by the destroyers *Lance* and *Landrail*, she was brought to action half an hour later. Then the destroyers *Lark* and *Linnet* joined in the chase, and by midday the other ships had come up. The enemy had evidently been badly damaged by our fire, for she was steaming away at a considerably reduced speed. At 12.15 she was in a sinking condition; so her crew abandoned her and jumped overboard. But her engines had not been stopped, and she still went on slowly until at last she turned round on her side and began to settle down. Out of the *Königin Luise's* complement of one hundred men, forty-three, some of whom were badly wounded, were picked up by our boats. Of these, twenty were taken into the *Amphion*.

The mine-layer had evidently been at work on the English coast, possibly even before the declaration of war; for at 6.35 on the following morning, August 6, the *Amphion* struck a mine. There was a violent explosion under the fore bridge. Every man on the fore mess-decks was killed, as were eighteen out of the twenty German prisoners in the ship. Captain Fox and the four officers on the bridge were stunned and badly burnt on hands and face. The *Amphion* now began to settle down by the head, and her sides forward were turning black as the result of the internal fires. For three or four minutes she continued to move slowly in a circle before the word could be given to stop the engines. The men all collected on the quarter-deck. There was absolutely no sign of panic. The boats were lowered quietly. The discipline was magnificent. Within a quarter of an hour after the explosion the boats from the destroyers were alongside the *Amphion*, and all the survivors were taken off.

After this had been safely effected, the fire that was raging under the fore mess-decks having reached the magazines, another terrific explosion occurred in the *Amphion*. This blew away a large portion of the fore part of the ship, and quantities of wreckage began to fall over the surrounding sea, causing several casualties in the destroyers. One shell fell on board the *Lark*, killing two men of the *Amphion*'s crew and a German prisoner who had just been rescued from the *Amphion*. Thus this man, who had survived two disasters in the space of a few hours, now fell a victim to the accident of falling debris.

It is worthy of mention that one of the destroyers' boats, while passing through the floating wreckage, came upon an uninjured football that had come from the *Amphion*. The men were keen on salving it; so it was picked up and brought on board the destroyer, and it was used throughout the following football season whenever the ship was in port. The Hun prisoners, belonging to a race that professes to despise the British for their love of sport, were given food for thought by this incident.

CHAPTER 2

The Heligoland Bight Action

The first naval action of the war was that in the Bight of Heligoland. In this the Harwich Forces played a notable part. The Harwich submarine flotilla under Commodore Roger Keyes (now Vice-Admiral Sir Roger Keyes) had a good deal to do with the preparation for the battle. At the beginning of the war these submarines were sent to guard the approaches to the English Channel, their object being to prevent any portion of the German fleet from passing through the straits and attacking the ships that were conveying our first Expeditionary Force to France. While thus employed they did valuable work in observing the movements of the enemy light forces in the North Sea. Acting on the information supplied by the submarines, the commander-in-chief decided to send the fast ships of the Harwich Force to make a sweep of the North Sea up to Heligoland and cut off enemy light craft known to be operating within that area.

August 28 was the day appointed for this raid. The Harwich submarines were sent out in advance to scout and to attack any enemy ships that might issue from the German bases to support their light craft. At the same time, from the Grand Fleet base, a squadron of cruisers was sent to the westward of Heligoland in order to intercept the German light craft should the Harwich Force succeed in cutting them out and driving them to the west. Beatty, with battle cruisers and light cruisers, went to an appointed position to be in readiness to support the Harwich Force when the time came. Probably one of the objects of this expedition was to entice the German capital ships to come out from their base and fight. If so, the expedition, though quite successful in its other aims, failed in that respect. For even at this early stage of the war the enemy refused to accept the challenge of the British Navy. The fighting took place within thirty miles of the German base. Within a very short time the enemy could have put an overwhelming force into action against our ships. But he did not do so, and allowed his light cruisers and destroyers to be sunk within hearing of his passive battleships and battle cruisers.

So on the morning of August 28 the Harwich Force, composed of two light cruisers—the *Arethusa*, Commodore Tyrwhitt's flagship, and the *Fearless*, commanded by Captain W. F. Blunt—with forty destroyers, were sweeping round towards Heligoland. This, of course, was very early in the war, and the *Arethusa*, a brand-new ship, had had no time to carry out her gun practice and complete other preparations when she was ordered out. At 4 a.m. the *Arethusa* and twenty of the destroyers were within seventy miles of Heligoland, sweeping down towards the island at twenty knots, the *Fearless* and the other twenty destroyers following five miles astern. The weather was fine, but when it is not rough in the North Sea it is usually misty, and it was so on this occasion, the visibility being only 5000 yards. Just before 7 a.m. an enemy destroyer appeared on *Arethusa*'s port bow. One of our destroyer divisions was ordered to chase her. This, as one who took part in the action put it, "started the ball." The fog lifted a bit, and the sun's rays occasionally broke through it. And now out of the mists ahead loomed several objects which proved to be enemy destroyers and torpedo-boats. It was evident that the Harwich Force had run into the patrols that it had been sent to seek out. A very brisk engagement was now fought between our destroyers and those of the enemy. In the course of this destroyer action, the 4th Destroyer Division, composed of the *Liberty*, *Laurel*, *Lysander*, and *Laertes*, engaged an enemy light cruiser and torpedoed her, but did not put her out of action. Both *Liberty* and *Lysander* were a good deal knocked about and had numerous casualties, the captain of the *Liberty* being among the killed.

A curious incident occurred at the close of this destroyer action. Another of our destroyer divisions had engaged and sunk an enemy destroyer. The British destroyer *Defender* had lowered a boat to save the survivors, who were struggling in the water. The boat had picked up several of the men, when a German light cruiser opened fire both upon our destroyers and upon the boat. The order came to the *Defender* and the other destroyers to retire at once, and this they had to do, leaving the boat behind. To the men in the boat the outlook was not a cheerful one. Imprisonment in Germany for the duration of the war seemed their probable fate. But the retirement of the enemy had by this time commenced, and the German light cruiser which had been shelling them now steamed away without stopping to pick them up. At this juncture, while the enemy light cruiser was still in sight, there popped up close to the boat the periscope of a submarine. The submarine rose to the surface, and to the delight of our men proved to be British—the *E4*, under the command of Captain E. W. Leir. She took off the British sailors and a few sample Huns, and, not having accommodation for more, left the other Germans in the boat, having first provided them with biscuit, water, and a compass.

It was ascertained afterwards that this boat never reached Heligoland, though that island was but a few miles distant and the weather remained fine. The probable explanation is that the Germans, recognising the English build of the boat, concluded that she contained British sailors, so sank it with gunfire and left the men to drown, as is the custom of the Huns.

And now to turn back to the flagship and the *Fearless* and the main force of destroyers, which were engaging the enemy destroyers and torpedo-boats. Shortly before 8 a.m. a German light cruiser was sighted on the *Arethusa's* port bow. The *Arethusa* at once attacked her; but the German was apparently unwilling to continue the fight and made away to the eastward.

But while the *Arethusa* was engaging her yet another German light cruiser, identified as the *Frauenlob*, appeared on the scene, and she was quite ready for a duel with her opposite number. The *Arethusa* engaged her closely, the two ships for a while steering on converging courses. The *Arethusa* at last closed the range to 3500 yards. The *Frauenlob's* fire was remarkably accurate. Within ten minutes the *Arethusa* was hit thirty-five times, with a loss of twelve killed, including the flag lieutenant, who was on the bridge, and twenty wounded. The *Arethusa* all the while was pouring in a deadly fire with her six-inch guns, and the *Frauenlob* must have been in a sorry plight. At last a six-inch shell, striking her on her bridge, knocked her out. For she at once turned and steamed away to the eastward as fast as she was able. A curious incident occurred in the course of this duel between the two ships. The *Arethusa's* cook, who at the time was in the galley preparing the men's breakfast—for a ship's domestic arrangements cannot be disturbed by battle—had one of his arms shot away. He might have bled to death, but, seeing an empty cigarette tin, promptly clapped it on the stump and so saved his life.

Heligoland, only five miles distant, now became visible, looming large through the mist. The *Arethusa* and the destroyers had accomplished their work, for the enemy light cruisers, destroyers, and torpedo-boats were all seen to be hurrying home. The Harwich Force, its object achieved, turned round and steered westward for England, for with crippled vessels the danger of remaining longer in enemy waters was, of course, very great. The *Arethusa* had been severely knocked about. All her torpedo tubes had been smashed. Her feed tank had been holed, and the engineer commander reported that he could now only get twelve knots instead of thirty out of her. The enemy had also employed shrapnel against her with such effect that her bridge and upper works were as indented as a nutmeg-grater; and on almost any part of her decks one could stoop and pick up a handful of shrapnel fragments, so thick they lay. But in a short time the ship had been cleared up, disabled guns had been repaired, and the casualties had been replaced by other men.

About one hour after the Harwich Force had turned and started for home, the *Arethusa*, limping along, picked up a wireless message from the destroyer *Lurcher*, attached to the Harwich submarine flotilla, reporting that she was being pursued by five enemy light cruisers off Heligoland. On receiving this message Commodore Tyrwhitt immediately turned back to support the *Lurcher*. The peril of taking such a course with a crippled flagship needs no explaining, but the old traditions of the sea make a commander very loth, in any circumstances, to refrain from going to the aid of a friend in difficulties. In the course of this war our ships have often thus hurried to the succour of others in the face of fearful odds. Over-rashness may have been displayed on occasion. But let us regard another side of the question. What confidence and spirit it must give to our men to feel that, if menaced by deadly peril, they can rely upon their comrades to come to their help if it is humanly possible to do so! A navy that has no soul, in which a commander will coldly calculate the exact risk before deciding whether the game is quite worth the candle, will never achieve great things.

So the flagship, the *Fearless*, and the two destroyer flotillas, having turned, steamed back to the eastward for one hour and were once more within a few miles of Heligoland. They found themselves on a sea empty of ships; no more wireless messages from the *Lurcher* reached the *Arethusa*, and as nothing could be seen or heard of that vessel, the quest was at last abandoned and the order was given to steam once more to the westward for home.

The mist now gradually thickened. At about 10 a.m., shortly after the squadron had turned, a light cruiser was seen coming out of the fog on the *Arethusa's* port quarter. For a second or so it was thought that she was one of our own ships. On being challenged she flashed some signals. Then a ripple of flame ran along her sides, and she displayed her true colours by opening fire on the flagship. The light cruiser *Fearless* and the destroyers, though they had but few torpedoes left, attacked her in a most gallant fashion and succeeded in driving her off. But, doubtless knowing that the *Arethusa* was in a crippled condition and that other German ships were coming up, she soon returned to resume the attack. And now another enemy light cruiser suddenly loomed on the *Arethusa's* starboard quarter and joined in the fight. The British ships were now fighting a retiring action, our destroyers doing splendid work, zigzagging over the sea and losing no opportunity of vigorously attacking the enemy, thus covering the retirement.

But now there came up on our squadron's front yet another enemy light cruiser, the *Mainz*, to take part in the action. So our ships were being attacked on all sides, and despite the bravery of the defence the situation must have appeared somewhat desperate. Our destroyers attacked the new arrivals, giving them no respite. The *Mainz* put up a great fight against the destroyers that were harassing her. Her fire was accurate; she put two of the destroyers out of action.

At this juncture there came up out of the mist our own 1st Light Cruiser Squadron, and with its assistance the *Mainz* was finished off and sunk. Shortly afterwards our battle cruiser squadron hove in sight. This brought the enemy's attack on our light force to an end, and the German ships turned and made for home. But they had fallen into a trap from which there was no escape. The *Arethusa*, after she had passed through our light cruiser squadron, came suddenly out of the fog into blue sky and glorious sunshine. Behind her to the eastward rose like a wall the dense fog-bank concealing all from view; but there was heard coming out of the fog-bank the roar of a tremendous cannonading. It was the roar of the guns of Beatty's ships which attacked and sank the remaining two German light cruisers.

The fight was over for the ships of the Harwich Force; they slowly steamed homeward, the *Arethusa* crawling ever slower, the salt water getting into her boilers, while such of our destroyers as had been badly damaged were being towed back. But none of the ships was lost; they all got safely into harbour. At 7 p.m. the *Arethusa* was compelled to stop her engines, and two hours later she was taken in tow by the *Hogue* and taken to Chatham, where I happened to be when she arrived. Looking at her battered condition, one wondered that her casualties had not been even heavier than they were. I wish that I could have supplemented this brief description with the narratives of some of the destroyer captains who had fought their ships so gallantly. Among other honours given, the D. S. O. was conferred on Captain W. F. Blunt, the captain of the *Fearless* light cruiser, in recognition of his repeated vigorous and dashing attacks on the enemy.

In the course of this action we had not lost a ship, and our ships that had been damaged were repaired and at sea again within a few weeks; whereas the enemy had lost three light cruisers and one destroyer, and withdrew with many ships badly damaged.

As for the *Arethusa*, her repairs were made good at Chatham, and a month later she was able to rejoin the Harwich Force. She had further adventures and narrow escapes, but her life, if stirring and most useful to her country, was a short one, and her end was tragic. In February 1916, only eighteen months after she had been launched, while returning from an attempt to intercept an enemy force, she was struck by a mine off Felixstowe, and her engines were disabled by the explosion, which killed eleven men in her boiler-room. A south-east gale was blowing and a high sea was running. Attempts were made to take her in tow, but the hawsers parted, and she drifted helplessly on to the Cutler shoal in a sinking condition. Her back was broken, and she fell in two.

A dreadful incident of this tragedy was the attempt of a stoker, maddened by pain, to escape from below by climbing up the inside of the funnel. He was seen appearing over the top of the funnel, and was helped down. His clothes had all been burnt off; his injuries were terrible, and he shortly afterwards died. The fate of the stokers trapped below, when disaster comes in this fashion, is a feature of naval warfare horrible to contemplate.

One of the *Arethusa's* stokers, by the way, must have been a very powerful sleeper. While the ship was breaking up and all the survivors—so it was supposed—had been taken off, a man appeared on a portion of the wreck, waving his hand for help. He was rescued, and proved to be a stoker, who had been sleeping below tranquilly through the explosion, the wreck, and the breaking up of the ship. It was only when he was awash and the water was pouring over his face that he woke to the situation.

CHAPTER 3

Other Actions

In the actions that were fought in the North Sea whenever the heavy ships of the enemy came out and encountered our own, the light Harwich Force played its part in harassing the enemy and in invaluable reconnaissance. In the battle of the Dogger Bank, January 28, 1915, its object was to sight the enemy battle cruisers and to put our own upon them. It will be remembered that on this occasion the German battle cruisers turned and hurried towards home as soon as they sighted our ships. The battle therefore resolved itself into a stern chase on the part of Admiral Beatty's fleet, which gradually gained on the enemy and closed the range. The enemy's destroyers covering the German retirement delivered vigorous attacks in order to delay the pursuit, but were driven back by our destroyers of the Harwich flotillas. When the German armoured cruiser *Blücher*, which had been damaged badly by our fire, dropped astern of the German line, the *Indomitable* was detached to finish her off, and while thus engaged was screened by the 1st Destroyer Division of the Harwich force. The *Arethusa* gave the *coup de grâce* to the *Blücher* with a torpedo and sank her. The *Arethusa* and the destroyers were picking up the survivors of the *Blücher* when a Taube flew overhead and attacked the boats with bombs, killing Germans struggling in the water as well as some of our own men. So the *Arethusa* recalled the boats. Otherwise more of the *Blücher's* crew might have been saved. The final duty of the Harwich Force on this occasion was to screen the *Indomitable* while she towed the disabled Lion back to the Grand Fleet base in the Firth of Forth.

During the Lowestoft raid of April 25, 1916, while the German battle cruisers were bombarding our coast, the Harwich Force did good work. The *Conquest*, flying the Commodore's pennant, the *Cleopatra*, and sixteen destroyers were sent out to distract the attention of the enemy and, if possible, torpedo some of his ships. While carrying out this duty they suffered severely. They sighted four enemy battle cruisers screened by light cruisers and destroyers. They made a vigorous attack upon this screening force, and this compelled the German battle cruisers, which at the time were bombarding Lowestoft, to cover their own light craft by turning their attention on the Harwich Force. The latter, now exposed to a heavy fire from the enemy big ships as well as from the light cruisers and destroyers, had to turn and retire.

It was while our ships were thus turning, and were, so to speak, bunched up in the loop formed by the turning operation, that they suffered severely from the enemy salvoes. The *Conquest* was hit by four or five twelve-inch shells, and lost forty-seven of her crew killed and wounded. Later, the *Penelope* was torpedoed by an enemy submarine. The explosion carried away her stern-post and rudder; the whole after part of her had practically been blown off. But she managed to steam back to Harwich at twenty-two knots, steering with her engines. Other ships also were hit. But the Harwich Force, at any rate, had drawn the fire of the Germans from Lowestoft, and so saved that town from a heavier bombardment than it received. The Huns, as was their wont in these raids, carried on the bombardment for half an hour or so, and then turned and hurried homewards as fast as they could steam, for they had no desire to encounter the ships from the Grand Fleet.

In the battle of Jutland the Harwich Force was not called upon to take a part. However, eight destroyers belonging to the Harwich Force had been detached to join Admiral Beatty before that action. These took part in the battle, screening the battle cruisers and delivering torpedo attacks. One destroyer, the *Turbulent*, was lost. Vessels of the Harwich Force, lent for the time to Sir Roger Keyes, also took part in the famous attack on Zeebrugge.

Among the many interesting minor actions fought by sections of the Harwich Force was that off the island of Texel on October 17, 1914. The light cruiser *Undaunted*, with the destroyers *Loyal*, *Legion*, *Lance*, and *Lennox*, while patrolling, sighted four German torpedo-boats, which turned away and endeavoured to escape when they realised that the ships approaching them were British. Our destroyers, which were screening the *Undaunted*, now changed their formation to single line ahead and gave chase. By 2 p.m. they were within range of the enemy, and by 3.20 they had sunk all four. First the two leading destroyers, *Lennox* and *Lance*, attacked and sank the leading enemy torpedo-boat. Then the destroyers, cutting in between the enemy ships, sank them in turn. During the action the *Undaunted* kept outside effective torpedo range and engaged the enemy at long range, attacking whichsoever ship happened to be nearest to her at the time. The enemy losses were very heavy; only forty-seven men were picked up by our boats, of whom many afterwards died of their wounds. On this occasion the enemy fought with great gallantry against a far superior force.

CHAPTER 4

The Convoys

The world is beginning to understand how successful was the British Navy in circumventing the enemy's submarine campaign, and so preserving this country from famine, while at the same time so closely blockading (so soon as our politicians permitted this) the enemy's coasts that Germany was isolated and her position became desperate. Our navy combines brains with bravery, and cunning indeed were some of the devices planned to outwit and trap the Hun. Of these devices but little is known outside the navy, and much probably never will be known, for there must be secrets well worth the keeping until the League of Nations or the millennium makes future wars impossible. Sir Arthur Conan Doyle, in a recently published, prophetic short story, written before the war, pictures vividly to us an England beaten, compelled to submit to an ignominious peace, by a very small power that makes unrestricted use of submarine warfare. He foresaw the danger, but thankfully acknowledges in his preface that he did not foresee the extraordinary ingenuity with which our navy overcame this danger.

Among its other functions, the Harwich Force, in a variety of ways, took an important part in this task of keeping the seas open to ourselves and closed to our enemies.

Firstly, to deal with that essential duty—the convoying of merchant vessels. This was part of the routine work of the destroyers of the Harwich Force. For some time the destroyers of the Force did all the escorting between Dover and Flamborough Head. They used also to convoy vessels along our East Coast, across the North Sea, and occasionally through the Straits down Channel to the westward. For example, throughout the war they kept open the traffic between England and Holland. This particular duty was known in the navy as the "Beef Trip," owing to the fact that in the first stages of the war the convoyed vessels were largely employed in the carrying of meat from Holland to England. It was a dangerous duty; enemy minefields had to be traversed, and the convoys were liable to be attacked by submarines, light craft, and seaplanes, for the Germans were ever on the lookout to intercept them.

The following method was pursued—and be it remembered that no lights were shown by destroyers or merchantmen. At night the destroyers and the mine-sweepers would pass through a swept channel off Orfordness to an appointed rendezvous outside, where they fell in with their convoy, which sometimes was made up of as many as twenty merchantmen, but more usually of about twelve. The destroyers now took up a position to protect the convoy, surrounding it on all sides. The merchantmen were then formed into a column, three abreast, and proceeded to steam across the North Sea, a flotilla-leader and a convoy-guide heading the column, another flotilla-leader following close astern, and the destroyers on either flank zigzagging about, and ever watchful for the appearance of an enemy. When the convoy, on the further side of the North Sea, approached the area that had been mined by the Germans, the formation was altered. The convoy formed in line ahead, the destroyers tucking themselves in, so to speak, as close to the line of merchantmen as possible. In this narrow formation, with the destroyer mine-sweepers and the converted merchantmen mine-sweepers leading the way, their paravanes over the stern set at twenty feet to cut adrift all the mines encountered, the convoy steamed across the deadly enemy minefield to the comparative safety of the Dutch territorial waters beyond. Here the merchantmen parted from their escort, and steamed to the ports for which they were bound. The escorting destroyers then picked up the westward-bound merchantmen that were awaiting them, and convoyed them back to the English coast, using the same formations that had been employed on the outward voyage.

At the beginning of the war the convoys of merchantmen were at times not punctual in arriving at the rendezvous on the Dutch coast, thus adding to the risk of discovery by enemy submarines. But before long the merchant captains understood what was required of them, and all went smoothly. It is scarcely necessary to say that the route followed across the North Sea and through the enemy's minefields was ever being changed, so as to lessen the chance of attack. When the risks attending these operations are taken into consideration, the casualties were few among the convoyed merchantmen. In the course of the war about six of them only were lost on this route. It is strange that none of the mine-sweepers that led the convoys and exposed themselves while clearing the way for the others fell victims to the mines. But, of course, the mine-sweepers that have been recently employed are of very shallow draught, and pass safely over most of the mines, especially at high water.

On the other hand, the escorting destroyers suffered heavily; several were sunk by mines or submarines, while still more were severely damaged. On one disastrous night in December 1917, three destroyers were lost while crossing the enemy's minefields with a convoy. First one destroyer struck a mine and was blown up. A second destroyer coming up to pick up the crew from the water struck another mine and also sank. A third destroyer then hurried to the rescue, only to share the same fate. Out of the three crews, only about one-fourth of the men were ultimately saved.

In this short summary of the doings of the Harwich Force in the war, it is not possible to describe a tithe of the heroic deeds performed by the men of that force, or to mention the names of those who performed them. But I have received a letter from a member of the crew of one of these three lost destroyers who signs himself, "A grateful survivor of that night," from which I propose to quote a few passages, for it exemplifies the spirit of the British Navy and the just pride that the "band of brothers" who fought under Tyrwhitt take in the

Harwich Force. I may say that eye-witnesses confirm all that my correspondent writes.

Four destroyers were on the scene, *Surprise, Torrent, Tornado* and *Radiant.* The last-named alone returned. The most gallant rescue-work was performed by the *Radiant,* under the command of Commander Fleetwood Nash, D. S. O., whose cool and skilful handling of his ship under dangerous conditions was the means of saving so many lives. Most gallant was the conduct of the sub-lieutenant and the men who went into the ice-cold water among the struggling and drowning men, at great risk to themselves, to save lives. Exceptional coolness, too, was displayed by the engine-room and stokehole branch of the *Radiant* while rescue work was being performed in the dangerous area. That all survivors volunteered, on their own, to serve in the Harwich Force, although some of them had been mined or torpedoed two or three times previously, speaks for the splendid type of men who man the ships of the Harwich Force.

The laying of mines and the destruction of one another's minefields used to keep the Germans and ourselves well occupied, and the scraps that occurred between craft engaged in these operations were very frequent. It was one of the regular duties of the Harwich Force to escort our own mine-layers and to protect our minefields—which extended across the Bay of Heligoland from Holland to Denmark—against the interference of enemy mine-sweepers.

The following will serve as an example of the encounters that so often took place. In August 1917 a section of the Force, which throughout the night had been supporting our own mine-layers (the latter had been busy laying mines on our minefield), on the following morning, while steaming close along the edge of the minefield in somewhat foggy weather, sighted about eight enemy mine-sweepers, undoing the night's work and energetically sweeping up our mines. The fire of our destroyers sank two of the mine-sweepers, and the others, though badly damaged, were enabled, owing to their light draught, to escape across the minefield, where our deeper craft could not follow. The mine-sweepers were escorted by destroyers and submarines, which did their utmost to torpedo our ships, but failed to accomplish their purpose. Sometimes, however, the enemy had better luck, as when they torpedoed the *Mentor* while she was escorting one of our mine-layers in the Heligoland Bight. A huge hole was blown right through the *Mentor*, from one side to the other. Fortunately, the sea was smooth, and she contrived to return home.

On the other hand, the enemy's mine-layers were ever being hunted down by the Harwich Force, and the sinkings of them were not few. The first incident of the war in the North Sea was the sinking of a German mine-layer off Lowestoft by the light cruiser *Amphion*. The story of the *Meteor* is worthy of note. This enemy mine-layer, disguised as an innocent old tramp, laid a number of mines in the Cromarty Firth. Having completed her work, she started on her homeward journey, but attracted the attention and suspicion of the captain of the *Ramsey*, the armed boarding steamer which lay off Cromarty. So he sent off a boat to board and question her. On this the *Meteor* let loose a torpedo and blew the *Ramsey* up. The *Meteor* got away safely, but her triumph was short-lived. The Harwich Force, which was patrolling on the Jutland coast, fell in with her, as she was nearing home, off Horn Reef, early in the afternoon. She was being escorted by two Zeppelins. As she could not escape from the British patrol, she blew herself up. On this occasion the Germans seem to have been caught napping; for at eight o'clock that morning enemy seaplanes had flown over our patrol and bombed it. The enemy therefore should have received early information of the approach of a British force, and it is strange that German ships, of which there were many within call, did not come out to support the *Meteor* and attack the patrol.

To our navy, an enemy on the surface is a welcome sight, for with him one can fight a fair fight. But the unseen mines of the enemy, lying in wait to bring about disaster in a second, are another matter. I imagine that there cannot be a sailor who does not curse the inventor of mines. It is true that we got our own back on the enemy with our own mines; but a good many ships of the Harwich Force have suffered from mines in the course of the war. In a large majority of cases the ships struck by mines did not sink, were got home, were repaired, and fought again. Some of our ships, now looking spick and span, with nothing to show that they have ever suffered, have been mined several times. The numerous watertight compartments into which a warship is divided keep her afloat even after terrible injuries.

Thus the *Centaur*, light cruiser, was mined in the Bight of Heligoland. The mine struck her forward, and so damaged her bows that her bulkheads would have given way had she attempted to steam ahead, so she steamed back across the North Sea stern first. The *Centaur* was mined on yet another occasion, during the great gale of October 1917. The Harwich Force had gone out to look for the enemy—on information received, as the police would say. A terrific westerly gale was encountered by the ships on their homeward voyage. All lost their topmasts, their wireless thus being put out of action. At noon, while the gale was at its worst, a loud explosion was heard on the *Centaur*—at that time the flagship of the Harwich Force. She had been badly mined aft. It must have been an anxious moment, for in such fearful weather her consorts could not have come to her assistance had she been totally disabled. One of her two condenser doors had been broken in by the concussion. Fortunately, the other door held, and she was enabled to steam home with one engine.

As an example of the way in which a naval ship can be mined and yet be little the worse for it, may be mentioned the case of a Harwich destroyer which struck a mine off Orfordness in April 1916. The explosion blew her stern off and threw her four-inch gun up into the air. It did not go overboard, but fell back upon her deck. No lives were lost; no one was even hurt. She got back to port, was repaired, and very soon was at work again.

CHAPTER 5

Escorting Seaplanes

The Harwich Force also took its part in the numerous air raids that were made from the close of 1914 onwards on the German mainland and islands. It was perilous work not only for the seaplanes but for the seaplane-carriers and the ships forming the escort; for, after the seaplanes had been launched and had flown away on their mission of destruction, these ships had to repair to an appointed rendezvous off the German coast, to there await (often for a long time and sometimes in vain) the return of the seaplanes and pick them up. A description of a few of these air-raid expeditions will illustrate this.

It will be remembered that British seaplanes bombed Cuxhaven on Christmas Day, 1914. On Christmas Eve a force consisting of the flagship *Arethusa*, another light cruiser, a flotilla of destroyers, and three seaplane-carrying ships, carrying the seaplanes, set out from Harwich in a northeast gale. It was a very dark night, and on nearing the further side of the North Sea the ships picked their way to their destination by the lead, following the line of ten-fathom soundings. At four in the morning they passed some outpost vessels, who doubtless detected them and signalled their presence to the enemy, for a great burst of German wireless was immediately observed. At dawn, on reaching the appointed position twelve miles to the north of Heligoland, they found themselves in a flat calm. The seaplanes were hoisted out, rose from the water at once, and flew off in the direction of Cuxhaven—probably to the relief of all concerned. For in the early days of the war our seaplanes were not so reliable as those which we employed later. They not infrequently refused to rise for a considerable time, and floundered about on the sea helplessly, causing a dangerous delay in enemy waters. The flotilla now steamed to an appointed rendezvous on the west side of Heligoland, and there awaited the return of the seaplanes. While they were thus waiting, our ships were attacked by enemy submarines, two Zeppelins, and two seaplanes.

But no enemy surface craft came up, though it was, of course, expected that the warning given by the outpost vessels would have brought the German ships out in force. On this occasion all the seaplanes returned safely and were picked up; and at noon the flotilla steamed back, with no casualties to report, to Harwich. The fact remains that the Harwich Force stayed within a radius of twenty miles from Heligoland from 5 a.m. to 12.30 p.m. without any attempt being made by the High Sea Fleet to molest it.

But our air-raiding expeditions did not always enjoy this good fortune. For example, what is known as the Sylt raid was attended with loss of ships and seaplanes. The objectives of this seaplane attack were the enemy Zeppelin sheds at Tondern, on the Slesvig mainland. It was a raid that might have led to great events, as the British and German battle-cruiser squadrons were both out on the North Sea at the time, the first to cover the raiding ships, the latter to attack them. But the great sea battle that might have been fought was not fought because the Germans so willed it, and retired behind the shelter of their minefields before Beatty could get at them.

At an early hour of the morning of March 25, 1916, the Harwich Force, consisting of the light cruisers *Cleopatra*, *Undaunted*, *Penelope*, and *Conquest* (*Cleopatra* flying the Commodore's pennant), a number of destroyers, and the seaplane-carrier *Vindex*, arrived off the west coast of Sylt Island. A short time before reaching the spot at which it was proposed to hoist out the seaplanes, the *Cleopatra*, screened by half the destroyer force, and leading the *Vindex*, proceeded in advance, leaving the rest of the force to await her return. When the selected spot was reached, the track of a torpedo was observed to be approaching the *Cleopatra*. It was avoided by turning towards and following its track.

The destroyers were now detailed to keep the German submarine down while *Cleopatra* and *Vindex* stopped to hoist out the five seaplanes. The morning had been bright, but a dense snowstorm came on shortly after the seaplanes had been hoisted out. However, the weather cleared for a while, and all the seaplanes had got away by 5.30 a.m. But further snowstorms that followed made the flying conditions very difficult, and the seaplanes lost their bearings while searching for their objective.

The *Cleopatra*, the *Vindex*, and the escorting destroyers now rejoined the remainder of the force at the appointed rendezvous, and awaited the return of the seaplanes. At 7 a.m. the first seaplane returned and was hoisted in, and a little later a second was picked up—the only two of the five that ever did come back.

As the time appointed for the return of the seaplanes had passed, and there were no signs of the others, the force proceeded in search of the three missing ones, the cruisers penetrating the channel inside the Horn Reef, while the destroyers were ordered to the south-east to spread out and get in as near as possible to the German coast, so that they might protect against enemy attack and pick up any damaged seaplanes that might arrive. The search was fruitless, but it led to various incidents.

The destroyers steamed in near enough to bombard the coast. Close under the shore, near the German harbour of List, they engaged enemy patrol vessels and aircraft. They sank two of the patrol boats (armed trawlers) and brought down a seaplane. While our boats were picking up survivors, some of these patrol boats threw out such dense clouds of smoke to screen themselves that, in the obscurity thereby caused, a collision took place between two of the British destroyers, the *Laverock* ramming the *Medusa* and holing her badly in the engine-room. The *Laverock*, despite her injuries, was able to proceed under her own steam, but the *Medusa* was wholly disabled.

In the meanwhile, urgent wireless messages from the admiralty were received ordering the Commodore to withdraw. To remain longer on the coast with a crippled ship in tow would be to invite the attack of a superior enemy force; in fact, it was known that strong forces were already putting to sea from the

German bases; so at 11 a.m. the Commodore ordered the entire force to withdraw to the westward. The flotilla-leader *Lightfoot* took the *Medusa* in tow.

At the beginning of the homeward voyage the enemy seaplanes circled round the ships, but were kept off by our high-angle guns. One plucky German airman, however, despite the shrapnel that was bursting all round him, made a most determined attack. He dropped about eight bombs and very nearly hit the *Conquest*. But the ever-increasing strength of the wind, and the signs of worse weather coming, at last made the German airmen turn to seek shelter on their own land.

The flotilla soon found itself steaming in the teeth of a strong south-west gale, violent rain-squalls alternating with snow-blizzards, and a high sea running. Progress was slow, for the speed of the flotilla was necessarily limited to that at which their crippled consort could be towed, and that speed, as the wind ever hardened, was gradually reduced from ten to only six knots.

At 4 p.m. the flotilla sighted ahead of it, steaming to the southward, the ships of Sir D. Beatty's squadron of cruisers that had been sent to support it. The delay caused by the wait for the seaplanes that did not return and by the crippled state of the *Medusa* had brought about a dangerous situation. The mission of the battle cruisers had been to cruise to the southwest and prevent the enemy from attacking the Harwich Force while the seaplane raid was in progress, and, at the conclusion of the raid, to cover the withdrawal of that force, by following it to the westward at a certain distance astern. Had all gone well, the battle cruisers should have had the Harwich Force well to the westward of them by 9 a.m., whereas it was only appearing in sight towards sundown. It was a serious matter to risk our valuable battle cruisers in covering the slow retirement, at night, through enemy waters, of a force retarded by its lame ducks. It was known that a large number of the enemy's torpedo craft were out to intercept our forces, and these would find easy targets in our big ships. But it had to be done, and the battle cruisers covered the passing of the Harwich Force through the danger zone.

To return to the Harwich Force. Shortly after the battle cruisers had been sighted, the Commodore altered the course to the north, thus considerably lessening the chance of our ships getting in touch with the enemy who were coming out of Wilhelmshaven or some other German base to the southward.

This alteration of course brought the wind and sea on the *Medusa*'s quarter, causing her to override repeatedly, and so put a great strain on the towing hawser each time that it tautened out. No hawser could stand this long, and it promptly parted. Further attempts were made, but it became obvious that to tow the *Medusa* home would not be possible. It was therefore decided to abandon her, and the order was given to take the crew off her and then to sink her. That this was a difficult and dangerous operation to carry out with so tremendous a sea running, and on so dark a night, needs no explanation. But it was done, and that, too, without the loss of a man, Lieutenant-Commander Butler, who was in command of the destroyer *Lassoo*, got his ship alongside the *Medusa*. In order to effect his purpose he had to ram the *Medusa* in the forecastle, and to continue steaming ahead so as to preserve contact with her until he had taken all her crew on board his own ship. It was a piece of magnificent seamanship, and Lieutenant-Commander Butler well earned the D. S. O. which was conferred on him.

So as to minimise the possibility of friend being mistaken for foe in so dark and stormy a night, with no ships showing lights, the destroyers were sent on in advance, while the light cruisers proceeded in line ahead, *Cleopatra*, the flagship, leading; the speed, now that the *Medusa* had been abandoned, being increased to fifteen knots. A northerly course was still steered by the force, but the *Lightfoot* and *Lassoo*, with the crew of the abandoned *Medusa*, were ordered to steam direct to Harwich.

Shortly after 10 p.m. a vessel steaming fast was sighted on *Cleopatra*'s port bow. Captain F. P. Loder Symonds, at that time in command of the *Cleopatra*, observing that showers of sparks were coming from this vessel's funnel, showing that she was burning coal and not oil fuel, rightly assumed that she was an enemy; so he put his helm hard a-starboard and went full speed ahead to intercept her. Very soon afterwards two destroyers were distinguished steaming across the *Cleopatra's* bow at right angles. Captain Loder Symonds promptly reversed his helm and steadied his ship to ram. There was about a boat's length only between the two destroyers. The leading destroyer just got clear; but the *Cleopatra* struck the second destroyer full amidships and practically at right angles. There was heard a violent explosion, a tremendous noise of escaping steam, and the crash of rending metal; and then it was seen that the *Cleopatra* had run right through the destroyer, cutting her in two. The two halves were seen drifting past the *Cleopatra*, one half on her port, the other on her starboard side. The *Cleopatra* then altered her course to attack the other destroyer, and both the flagship and the *Undaunted*, which was the cruiser next astern to her, opened fire; but the enemy escaped, quickly disappearing in the darkness. The sinking of the German destroyer through the prompt decision taken by Captain Loder Symonds is recognised by those who were present as having been a remarkably fine piece of work on his part.

The rapid turnings of the flagship during her attack on the enemy destroyers were naturally carried out at considerable risk of collision with the light cruisers that were following her. The *Undaunted*, the next in the line, did run into the *Cleopatra* with sufficient force to partly cripple herself. So she was ordered to leave the line and steam to the Tyne.

Early in the following morning it was definitely known that the enemy battle cruisers had come out; so by 9 a.m. the Harwich Force, in accordance with orders, had joined our own battle cruiser fleet, and with it swept to the southward again in the hope of meeting the enemy. But the German big ships were not to be tempted into giving action, and withdrew to their base before our ships could get near them.

Accordingly, at 1 p.m. Admiral Beatty's battle cruisers turned to the north, bound for their base, while the Harwich Force steered directly for Harwich, which was reached that evening without the occurrence of any further incident. In the course of the operations we had lost one destroyer and three seaplanes, but the enemy had lost one destroyer, two armed patrol boats, and one seaplane. Probably some damage was also inflicted on the enemy by our seaplanes, for during the raid a German wireless message from some shore station was intercepted by the *Cleopatra*, to the effect that a bombardment was in progress.

It will be remembered that a subsequent air raid, which was carried out by a squadron from the Grand Fleet in the summer of 1918, on the same Zeppelin sheds at Tondern which were the objectives of the Sylt raid, was attended with complete success. The sheds were wrecked by the bombs from our aircraft, and two Zeppelins were destroyed.

As our air raids became more frequent the vigilance of the enemy submarines increased. Many were the narrow escapes of our escorts. Thus, in January 1916, the *Arethusa*, with some destroyers, was escorting the seaplane-carrier *Vindex* to the mouth of the Ems river. Just before dawn the vessels stopped in order that the seaplanes might be hoisted out. The first intimation that enemy submarines were about was the track of a torpedo racing at the *Arethusa* through the darkness. The torpedo passed right under the *Arethusa*'s ram, missing it by very little. A second torpedo followed, which was avoided by prompt use of the helm. So the flagship was saved, but only to be mined and sunk within sight of her base a few weeks later.

Our ships, as I have shown, always stood by a consort in distress, and brought her safely back to her base if it were possible to do so, even at the greatest risk to themselves; and there always was a great risk of envelopment and destruction by a superior force whenever a disabled ship was being slowly towed through enemy waters. Our crippled ships of the Harwich Force were never allowed to fall into the enemy's hands. Many are the stories of the saving of our ships in the North Sea during the war.

Let us take, for example, the case of the *Landrail*. In May 1915, off Borkum, while the seaplanes were being hoisted out from the seaplane-carrier for a raid on the German coast, one of the usual dense North Sea fogs rolled up. While the ships were shrouded in this, the light cruiser *Undaunted* was run into by the destroyer *Landrail*. The *Landrail*'s bows were smashed in, practically telescoped. In a photograph taken shortly afterwards she presented an extraordinary appearance, a large portion of her forward deck hanging over the wreckage where once had been her stem, like an apron. She was towed from Borkum to Harwich stern first. During the voyage heavy weather came on. She parted wire hawser after hawser, until there could have been few hawsers left on board the ships that were convoying her. Destroyer after destroyer, the *Mentor, Aurora*, and others, took her in tow in turn as the hawsers parted; and, finally, the *Arethusa* brought her in. Fog in war-time is not the least of the perils in the North Sea, and, considering the nature of the work that had to be carried on, fog or no fog, it is wonderful that collisions were not more frequent.

CHAPTER 6

The Patrols

In their indiscriminate warfare against merchantmen and fishermen the Germans generally sank our vessels (being unable to carry them into their own ports across the seas which our navy so well guarded), often leaving the crews to drown, and on many occasions disgracing their flag—which will ever be regarded as a symbol of dishonour among the nations—by firing at helpless men struggling in the water. When we captured an enemy merchantman we did not waste valuable material by sinking her, but brought her as a prize into one of our ports, while we treated the captured crews even too well. But our captures were not many after we had swept up such vessels as were upon the seas at the opening of the war; for, later, our command of the sea confined the enemy merchantmen within their own ports, and the North Sea was practically clear of them.

The destroyers of the Harwich Force, however, used to make successful raids on the enemy trawlers fishing in German waters, generally on the Jutland coast. It was the practice of our destroyers to spread out on nearing territorial waters, sweep in and drive the trawlers out, and then reassemble with their captures at an appointed spot. Prize crews were then placed on the trawlers, and they were sent to England. In one raid in 1915 over twenty were thus captured. Those that contrived to escape under the shore among shallows, where the destroyers could not follow, were sunk by our gun-fire.

Throughout the war the activities of the Harwich Force were unceasing, and took a variety of forms. A detachment would go out with the object of enticing the enemy over our submarines, which were lying below the surface awaiting them. There were patrols that were watching to intercept the Zeppelins and other aircraft that were crossing the North Sea to bomb our undefended cities. Sections of the force were lent to Dover to patrol off Ostend and Zeebrugge. It was while she was engaged on this latter duty that the *Cleopatra* was mined, but happily not lost. There were continuous patrols along the Dutch coast and the Frisian Islands to watch for and intercept the German naval forces that were attempting to make the Belgian ports. On many a stormy winter's night the destroyers would rush out in the teeth of the icy spray to attack a foe or assist a friend in difficulty. It was perpetual vigilance, peril, and sometimes toil almost beyond the endurance of human flesh. Thus, on one occasion two light cruisers had no sooner returned with their weary crews from a harassing three days' patrol, than they were ordered out again to cross the North Sea and reconnoitre the German High Sea Fleet, which, it was known, was coming out to manoeuvre off Heligoland. Thus people in England were enabled to sleep in their beds in confidence; for the unceasing patrols saw to it that no serious attack could be made on our coasts without ample warning being given.

At the beginning of the war—as all the world now knows—the number of our destroyers in the North Sea was wholly insufficient, the enemy being there far stronger than we were in these indispensable craft. Consequently it became incumbent upon the destroyers of the Harwich Force to perform duties which would have provided ample work for twice their number. After the war had started, of course, the construction of destroyers was carried on at a feverish speed in our shipyards, and now there is no lack of them.

But the activities of the Harwich destroyers were extended far beyond the limits of the North Sea. At the beginning of the war, for example, a division of destroyers from Harwich had Newport in Wales for its base, and was constantly employed in patrolling, screening big ships at sea, fighting submarines, convoying in the Atlantic, and so forth.

I will give a few details to show the sort of work that was done by the Harwich Force at the eastern approaches to the Channel. Through the winter of 1916-1917 there was always a division of the Harwich Force patrolling the Channel barrage in conjunction with the Dover Patrol. It was a one-month patrol. There was no leave, no short notice, and the ships only returned to Harwich for boiler-cleaning.

One important duty of the Harwich Force was to patrol the mine-net barrage which extended along the Belgian coast, parallel to and at about ten miles distance from the shore, from Dunkirk to Holland. There was nearly always one division of the Harwich Force, consisting of four destroyers, with one or two monitors, patrolling just outside the barrage by day, within effective range of the German guns on the shore (their range was 30,000 yards). By night the division used to patrol and protect the Downs. This patrol, based on Dover, used to carry on this work for three weeks at a stretch, always at sea, or ready to get off at a moment's notice. Its function outside the mine-net barrage was to prevent enemy submarines from passing through the barrage, and to stop the enemy destroyers from leaving their base. This channel patrolled by our destroyers was bordered on its south side by the mine-net barrage and on its north side by our minefields. On the further side of the minefields our light cruisers and destroyers patrolled in support.

Our destroyers had frequent scraps with the enemy across the narrow mine-net barrage. It was while engaged in this work that the Harwich Patrol co-operated with the Dover Patrol in the bombardment of the coast. On one occasion, at daylight, the Harwich Force sighted four German destroyers making for Zeebrugge. The *Centaur*, at that time Admiral Tyrwhitt's flagship, with other cruisers and destroyers of the Harwich Force, sank one of the enemy destroyers, the *S20*, and badly damaged other destroyers.

In the course of the execution of this duty of ever keeping a watchful eye on the enemy, the Harwich Force had its full share of fighting. Thus, on January 22, 1917, a calm, cold, very dark night, three of the light cruisers were on the lookout to intercept German destroyers that were known to be making for Zeebrugge. As they were steering in a south-westerly direction eight enemy destroyers were sighted passing close under their stern. A general mêlée followed at short range, 1000 yards and less, the cruisers blazing away with their guns, the destroyers replying with their torpedoes. One who took part in the action says that the atmospheric conditions helped to make the scene an extraordinary one. The enemy destroyers, as they rapidly turned hither and thither in their manoeuvring across the limited space which the action occupied, had their funnels crowned with a vivid red glow, and the smoke from them hung like a scarlet canopy over the engaging ships. The enemy ships must have been badly knocked about, for they soon retired, enveloped in a dense cloud of smoke. One was sunk in full view of our ships, and one at least was so damaged that she sank later. About an hour afterwards British destroyers fought a short action with the same enemy destroyers. Soon another of the enemy was seen to be hurrying to the Dutch coast, apparently in a sinking condition. During this action, so close was the fighting that one British destroyer and a German T. B. D. were engaged within pistol range of each other. The German escaped in the darkness, and had to put into Ymuiden in a terribly damaged condition. In this fight one of our destroyers, the *Simoon*, was blown up by an enemy shell which exploded in her fore magazine.

It would take long to tell the whole heroic story of the Harwich Force during the great war. At Harwich, the people, who are in close touch with the navy, and must know many things over which, hitherto, "Dora" has drawn her discreet veil, speak in terms of the profoundest admiration, pride, and respect of the officers and men of the light force which played its part so gallantly in defending the inviolability of England. Commodore Tyrwhitt—since 1917 Rear-Admiral Sir Reginald Tyrwhitt—was the right man to lead such men. And how wonderful have been his experiences throughout this long war! He has fought in many actions; in his successive flagships he has been torpedoed and mined—his first flagship, as we have seen, sank under him; he was ever cruising about enemy waters; he was ever finding himself in tight corners; and he always contrived to extricate his squadron from the most difficult situations.

PART 2

The Harwich Submarine Flotilla

CHAPTER 7

Composition of the Flotilla

The Submarine Flotilla at Harwich, acting as a separate unit and receiving its orders directly from the admiralty, though also at times working in co-operation with the Harwich Force of light cruisers and destroyers, played a very useful part in the naval war, and was especially instrumental in making the North Sea too uncomfortable for German submarines. At the commencement of the war the *Maidstone* was the only depot ship of the flotilla, but later she was joined by two others, the *Pandora* and the *Forth*, while another ship, the *Alecto*, was stationed as a branch depot ship at Yarmouth, that port being somewhat nearer the usual objective of our submarines than Harwich.

At the opening of the war, Commodore Roger Keyes was in command of the flotilla. Then Captain Waistell was in command until the end of the third year of the war. He was succeeded by Captain A. P. Addison, who is still in command. The average strength of the flotilla was eighteen submarines, the large majority of them being of the very useful "E" type. This was the only organised flotilla existing in England at the opening of the war. It had the advantage, therefore, of taking to itself all the senior and most experienced submarine officers in the navy, a fact that may account for the large percentage of hits made by the torpedoes of these submarines in the course of the war—a percentage of which officers and men naturally feel proud. At first the personnel of the flotilla comprised naval men only; but, later, numbers of men from the merchant service and artificers from shore works were absorbed into it. These latter became very keen and efficient, and are spoken of in terms of high praise by the officers.

It was the practice, when the submarines returned after one or other of their adventurous voyages, at once to remove the crews from their confined quarters to the depot ships, in which they lived until the time came to put to sea again. But as the war progressed the accommodation afforded by the depot ships became inadequate. Consequently the *Maidstone* and other depot ships which had been moored in the harbour were brought alongside Parkeston quay; while, facing the quay, on the ground that had been taken over from the Great Eastern Railway Company (a company, by the way, which co-operated with the admiralty in a zealous and patriotic fashion), there rapidly rose an extensive shore establishment, with storerooms, workshops, offices, and comfortable quarters for the submarine crews, who lived here instead of in the depot ships when their craft were in port.

The arrangements made for the comfort of the men were excellent. A church, a chapel, recreation rooms, a theatre, a cinema house, and canteens fronted the quay, and good companies were brought from London theatres and music-halls to entertain the sailors, while, of course, provision was also made for outdoor sports and games. There were, naturally, serious-minded people who considered that some of these arrangements were of a frivolous character, out of harmony with the tragedy of war. But those who organised these things knew better. The strain of submarine work is very great. To occupy the minds of the men with amusements while they are resting awhile on shore after their trying duties cannot but help to keep up their morale. And that the morale of the submarine men was wonderful all are agreed. Surely no other Service on land or sea can supply a greater test of sustained valour than does this submarine warfare. The conditions of it are uncanny, calculated to terrify the imagination. As a rule the submarine is playing a lone hand upon the seas. It is rare, when disaster comes, for a friendly ship to be near her to bring help or to carry tidings of her to England. In the great majority of cases, when one of our submarines has been lost, all that is known of the disaster is that she does not come home. What has happened to her remains a secret of the sea never to be revealed. An ordinary patrol for a submarine of the Harwich Flotilla was of about ten days; a mine-laying trip, of from three to six days' duration. When the overdue ship did not return there was suspense for several days, until at last it was realised that there was no longer room for hope.

In this little flotilla of eighteen submarines, ships that disappeared had to be replaced by others. For in the course of the war twenty "E" boats, two "D" boats, and one "L" boat belonging to the flotilla were lost, and these figures do not include the submarines that were detached from the Harwich Flotilla to be lost in the Mediterranean and Baltic. The sailor of to-day has not all the superstitions of his forefathers, but, like most people, he has some belief in omens. Certain coincidences made him regard it as very unlucky to sail in a submarine when a new captain was making his first voyage in her. Within a short period four submarines that had sailed out of Harwich under new captains were never heard of again. It was also recognised that ill luck was likely to attend the first voyage of a newly launched submarine; but that, so soon as the first voyage had been safely accomplished, all was well with the ship, which would then be faced only by the ordinary chances of war.

To turn to an amusing example of the superstition of the sea. In the course of one cruise a submarine of the Harwich Flotilla had fired seven torpedoes at various enemy ships without result. The captain discovered one of his crew kneeling on the deck over a bucket of sea-water. He was holding under the water and mercilessly wringing an object against which he was directing a volume of abuse in terms frankly nautical. Disgusted at the failure of the torpedoes, he was drowning the ship's mascot, a teddy bear or similar doll, hoping to change the luck. I wish that I could state that the next torpedo fired sank a Hun battleship, but I have no record of the sequel.

Even in war there are humorous incidents, and, indeed,

there are many of them. One submarine captain of this flotilla attacked a German submarine on the surface and gave chase to her with the intention of torpedoing her. But the Hun had the greater speed; the British submarine had no gun, and could not get near enough to the receding foe to use a torpedo. So the captain had to content himself with signalling insulting messages to the Hun, hoping to taunt him into fighting; but the shocked Hun dived under the surface and disappeared in order to avoid the language.

On another occasion a submarine of this flotilla and a German submarine passed very close to each other in such foul weather that nothing could be done in the way of fighting, so the two captains waved their hands cheerily at each other and went their respective ways. This is the only instance that I can recall of any Hun having displayed anything remotely resembling a sense of humour in the course of this war.

Our submarine commanders appear to have been adepts in the art of successfully bluffing the enemy when the occasion arose. For example, after one of our air raids on the German coast, a submarine of the Harwich Flotilla went to the rescue of one of our seaplanes that had fallen disabled to the water. While she was engaged in sinking the seaplane and taking off her pilot, a German aircraft came over very close. The captain of the submarine waved his cap to the enemy airmen, who concluded that the submarine was a German boat which had brought down an English seaplane and was capturing her pilot. As soon as the captain of the submarine had completed his task he dived quickly. The German must have then realised too late that he was dealing with an enemy, for as the submarine was moving away beneath the surface there was felt the shock caused by the bursting of bombs dropped by the Hun aircraft.

On another occasion, in June 1915, one of the Harwich submarines, on coming to the surface somewhere near the German coast, found that her engines were partly disabled. There was a German trawler in sight, and within range of the submarine's gun. The trawler would certainly have made a bolt for it, and in all probability would have got safely away, had she known that the submarine was incapable of giving chase to her. But the captain of the submarine induced the German to surrender and compelled him to tow the crippled submarine across the North Sea back to Harwich, where the trawler and her crew of eight men were handed over to the authorities.

CHAPTER 8

Reconnaissance and Mine-Laying

The principal duties of our submarines in the North Sea were reconnaissance, attack on the enemy's ships, especially on his submarines, and mine-laying. The Germans were the first to introduce the system of laying mines with submarines, but we quickly followed their example and constructed submarines for this purpose. One of our submarines carries about twenty mines. The weapon of our submarines is, of course, the torpedo, of which an "E" boat carries ten. Our submarines, unlike the German, usually carry nothing heavier than the twelve-pound gun. But towards the end of the war we were constructing submarines with heavier armament. Our latest "M" boat is armed with a twelve-inch gun; she was despatched to the Mediterranean, but the armistice was signed, and prevented her from showing what she could do in the war.

For reconnaissance work in the North Sea our submarines were invaluable, for they could patrol close under the enemy shores, seeing much without being seen themselves, and could do what surface ships could not do—remain there on the watch for several days at a time if necessary, for they were able to dive and disappear if detected and in serious danger. The submarines of the Harwich Flotilla had often to travel under our own and the enemy minefields. They were ever patrolling our own great minefields on the east side of the North Sea, and sending home wireless information as to the movements of the enemy light forces, and reporting any mine-sweeping operations on the part of the enemy that seemed to indicate preparations for a sortie. It was the ambition of every British submarine captain, by giving timely notice, to bring about what the Huns used to term "The Day," that is, an action between their somewhat over-shy capital ships and our own.

It was regarded as being of so great importance to obtain the earliest possible warning of Hun activities in the North Sea that an order was issued by the admiralty to the effect that a submarine on lookout patrol had for her primary duty to come to the surface and send home, by wireless, information as to *outward*-bound enemy surface craft; while her secondary duty was to attack. In the case of *homeward*-bound enemy surface craft, the primary duty was to attack. If there should be any doubt as to the destination of an enemy surface craft, it was the duty of the submarine first to report by wireless and then to attack.

I have already shown how, during the critical eight days that saw our First Expeditionary Force cross the Channel to France, the Harwich submarines kept a sleepless watch on the German coast, to attack the enemy ships should they come out to interfere with the transport of our troops. I have also explained that these submarines had a good deal to do with the preparation for the action in Heligoland Bight.

It was the *E23*, too, of this flotilla that, while patrolling, sighted the German High Sea Fleet on August 19, 1916. She first wirelessed home the news that the Germans had come out, and then delivered a bold attack. She torpedoed the battleship *Westphalen* on the port side. The result of the explosion gave the battleship a big list, but for a while she still went on with the battle fleet. As the list increased, she at last left the line and turned for home, escorted by destroyers. Thereupon the *E23* set out to intercept her, passed through the screen of enemy destroyers that were zigzagging round the *Westphalen*, and torpedoed her on the starboard side. The battleship contrived to get away, but in so damaged a condition that she must have been out of the war for a considerable time.

The strategical position occupied by the Harwich Flotilla also imposed upon it another duty of great responsibility. The submarines had to be ever ready to go south at a moment's notice to cover the eastern approach to the English Channel against the enemy capital ships, should these attempt to break through. Had the Germans made the attempt in earnest, there is no doubt that they would have had to pay a very heavy toll.

Admiral Sir David Beatty put it well when, in a speech delivered in Edinburgh, he spoke of our "submarine sentinels who carried out the same services as the storm-tossed frigates of Cornwallis off Brest."

The only British submarines that were adapted for the laying of mines were those of the Harwich Flotilla. Consequently, for a considerable time plenty of arduous, perilous work among the minefields fell to their lot.

The mine-laying submarines of the Harwich Flotilla were especially busy on the eastern side of the North Sea, where our great minefields were. Captains of submarines describe this portion of the sea as an ideal one for submarine work; for the depth of the water is generally of from twenty to thirty fathoms, at which depth a submarine can lie comfortably at the bottom without being subjected to an excessive pressure. Comfortable is, of course, a relative term. Most people would never be anything but extremely uncomfortable in the atmosphere of a submarine after she has been submerged for some hours. A fresh-air crank would die in it.

The great minefield which was declared by our government in the summer of 1917, the preparation of which was a gigantic undertaking, extended from the Frisian Islands to about latitude 56 degrees north. The Dutch, for their own purposes, removed their lightships from their coasts to the western side of this minefield, thus forming a line of lights running north and south, roughly along the 4th degree of east longitude. This our sailors facetiously named Piccadilly Circus. It was the business of the submarines to lay mines on the eastern part of this minefield, that is, near to the coast. Our surface mine-layers laid their mines further seaward; while still further west our large mine-laying ships, one of which can carry as many as three hundred mines, laid their mines just inside Piccadilly Circus. Our submarines used to patrol regularly along Piccadilly Circus to look out for and attack enemy ships, and at intervals went shorewards through the minefield in order to reconnoitre.

A mine-laying submarine used to adopt the following methods. She would get close under the enemy coast under cover of the night and then dive, to remain at the bottom until the morning. As soon as there was light enough she would rise until her periscope was above the surface, and ascertain her position by cross bearings of the shore taken through her periscope. Then she would move to the different positions at which she had to lay her mines, all the while using her periscope for the taking of cross bearings. When she had completed her work she would return home by night, travelling on the surface as before.

The patrolling submarines were bombed constantly by enemy Zeppelins and seaplanes, but with little effect. To the submarine the mine was by far the greatest danger, and no doubt the depth charge too accounted for some of our casualties. But, as I have said, in nearly all cases when a submarine is lost, no one knows what has happened. She merely does not come back. The mine-laying of the Harwich submarines was chiefly directed against the enemy submarines, the mines being generally laid at about eight feet below the surface, so as to catch these craft while travelling on the surface. They were also laid at forty feet or more, so as to strike the submarines when travelling under water.

The Harwich Flotilla certainly did its full share of the work that made the North Sea too dangerous for the enemy pirates. Latterly the German submarines, in their anxiety to reach waters where they could carry out their operations in conditions of less danger, endeavoured to escape from the North Sea as quickly as possible, travelling on the surface. Many of these fell victims to our mines, and, if they dived, to our depth charges. During the first months of 1918 the British Navy definitely got the better of the submarine enemy, and so many German submarines did not return to their base that panic seized the sailors who manned the "U" boats. We hear strange tales now of submarine crews that refused to join their ships, and of press-gangs that were sent to sweep up what men they could find in the brothels and taverns of a German seaport before the ship could put to sea.

One of the duties of the submarines of the Harwich Flotilla was to watch for and attack the enemy submarines as they attempted to escape from the North Sea by one or other of the two swept channels used by them for this purpose, one channel being carried from Heligoland in a north-westerly direction, the other one running close under the Frisian Islands. Ingenious traps were laid for the enemy; they were allowed no respite. It was in vain that they frequently changed the direction of their channels. No sooner had they prepared a new channel across the minefields than our alert submarines discovered it and blocked it with mines.

Some figures given by Sir Eric Geddes the other day show how effective was the work done by our submarine mine-layers. During the first six months of 1918 over a hundred German boats were caught by the mines laid by our submarines off the German North Sea coast, and in one month alone the mine barrier across the Channel below Ostend trapped seventeen German submarines. On the other hand, the Germans also were very vigilant. Their Zeppelin patrols, especially during last summer, were efficient, and were successful in discovering the position of the channels which we had swept across the German minefields.

There can be no doubt that the Zeppelins were of considerable service to the Germans in the North Sea; not that they did much damage with the bombs that they dropped—indeed, I have heard of one instance only of a bomb falling on a ship of the Harwich Force—but for a time our patrols were persistently followed by these scouting aircraft, flying overhead out of range of our guns, signalling our movements to the Huns. To our submarines working on the further side of the North Sea they were also a source of trouble, for over there the sea is much clearer than on our side, and a submarine below the surface is, as a rule, easily to be distinguished by a Zeppelin hovering above it. Before the end of the war, however, the activities of the Zeppelins were much reduced by the action of our own aircraft.

The fact remains that, in the long struggle between the German and British submarines in the North Sea, the work done by the latter was the most efficient and destructive, and broke the nerve of the enemy submarine crews, whereas the morale of our men remained unshaken to the end. The men of the soulless German Navy were brave enough at first, with the bravery inspired by an ineffable conceit and arrogance. They had been taught that the German Navy was in every respect superior to the British—in ships, guns, personnel, and skilful leadership. It had been impressed upon their submarine crews that within a few months the unrestricted piracy of the German submarine would bring England to her knees. Undeceived at last, they lost heart, and the submarine crews were the first to set the example of mutiny to the German Navy, the first to refuse to face the enemy that they had been taught to despise.

Later, the crews of the High Sea Fleet followed the example set by the submarines. When at last, after long waiting, that fleet was ordered to put to sea and make a fight of it, the ships' companies would not obey their officers, and the fleet had to remain in port. Our navy had no spectacular victory; there was no knock-out blow; for the enemy had had enough of it and threw up the sponge.

Chapter 9

Fine Submarine Records

That the patrolling and mine-laying on the enemy coast was work of a highly dangerous nature goes without saying. The first of our mine-laying submarines was launched in 1916 and joined the Harwich Flotilla. The new experiment was watched with great interest by naval men, but the history of that ship seemed of evil augury for the future of these craft. On her first voyage something went wrong, and she returned to port three days overdue, having caused much anxiety as to her fate. From her second trip she never returned.

While it is seldom that anything is known of the fate of our lost submarines, numerous are the records of the narrow escapes from destruction. It was not at all unusual, for example, when diving off the German coast, for a submarine to find herself in difficulties among the shoals. Thus one of the Harwich submarines, when diving close to the mouth of the Ems river, struck a sandbank with her stem, and slid up it until her conning-tower was well out of the water. Here she stuck firmly. At this critical moment two German destroyers were seen to come out of the Ems and approach her. Efforts were made in vain to wriggle her off the bank, and it looked much as if she would be numbered among our submarines that did not come back. But, as luck would have it, the Germans passed by without perceiving her. Ultimately, assisted by a rising tide, the submarine was got off the bank stern first, bumped along the bottom to the safety of deeper water, and lived to tell the tale and fight another day.

On Christmas Day, 1914, one of our small submarines, the

S1, forming part of the submarine force that was acting in conjunction with the Harwich Force during the Cuxhaven air raid, found herself in a perilous position. While diving to the bottom early that morning she struck an obstacle and knocked off her forward drop-keel. Relieved of this heavy weight, she shot to the surface. The order was given to fill her empty tanks with sea-water; but this failed to destroy her buoyancy, and it was found impossible to bring her below the surface. To remain with a submarine that refused to sink, so near to the enemy shore, was to invite disaster; so the only thing possible was done. The *S1* recrossed the North Sea as fast as she was able, and fortunately reached Harwich without encountering the enemy.

On one occasion *E31* came across a disabled Zeppelin—which earlier in the day had been winged by light cruisers of the Harwich Force—sitting on the water. The Zeppelin showed fight; she was sunk by the submarine's gunfire, and the survivors, seven in number, were taken off as prisoners. During the night, on the homeward voyage, the submarine was overtaken by a German light cruiser, which opened fire on her. "*Ach*, zey com!" triumphantly exclaimed one of the prisoners, a sulky German officer, who up till then had not uttered a word. The order had been given to dive, but for some reason this could not be effected quickly. Delay was dangerous, so the officer of the watch put the submarine's helm hard over, and she went round in circles, presenting a difficult target. The German cruiser now proceeded to steam round in still larger circles. For a while she was so close to the submarine that she could not get her guns to bear on her. Then she attempted to ram her, but in vain. Eventually the *E31* dived, and, just before her stern went under, she was struck in the after casing by a six-inch shell. When she had sunk she released some oil, and the Germans, seeing this, reported her as lost. But she was not much damaged, and got home. This throwing out of oil from a diving submarine was a ruse employed by both sides, and soon the appearance of a volume of oil upon the surface of the sea was no longer accepted as proof of a successful hit. But at any rate it left the other side in doubt as to what had happened.

Several submarines of the Harwich Flotilla have fine records to show. Take the *E9*, for example. She was the first of the flotilla to send an enemy ship to the bottom. Within a few weeks of the declaration of war she was lying off Heligoland, at times within three miles of it, on the watch for enemy ships to come out. She was rewarded by seeing the German light cruiser *Hela* steaming out of the harbour. She torpedoed and sank her. Next we hear of the *E9* awaiting her prey at the mouth of the Ems river. Her main object at the time was to report any sortie of the German heavier ships to our own cruisers, which were then at sea. Here she caught a German destroyer and torpedoed her. The destroyer broke in two, one half of her sinking to the bottom, while the forward half, being air-locked, sank to a certain depth only, and there remained with the bow sticking up above the surface. Later in the war the *E9* was detached from the Harwich Flotilla for service in the Baltic, and there her exploits were numerous. She sailed under sealed orders, and her instructions were to get into the Baltic as soon as possible. So she did not waste time by stopping to fight on her way. Thus, when passing through the Sound on a very dark night, she was nearly run down by a German destroyer. After the two ships had passed each other the submarine dived, so as to avoid the enemy's attentions. But the water was shallow and her periscope was still above the surface when she touched bottom. However, she escaped after bumping along the seafloor for four hours before she found herself in deeper water. In the Baltic she sank two destroyers and torpedoed and badly damaged a third. She sank two German transports while they were being escorted by cruisers. Next she torpedoed a large ship, which looked like a battleship of the Deutschland class, coming out of Danzig. She was probably supporting the fleet that was then attacking the Russians. The ship apparently was severely damaged by the torpedo, and volumes of smoke were seen to be pouring from her. *E9* also sank four German merchantmen which were running iron ore from Sweden to Germany. The submarine boarded them, put charges in them, and blew them up. I need not say that no German lives were lost on this occasion, for the submarine was flying the British flag. Ultimately, when the Russian revolution broke out, the *E9*, with other ships, were blown up by us in the Gulf of Finland, to prevent them from falling into the hands of the enemy.

E16, of the Harwich Force, also had a fine record. Among other exploits, she sank a destroyer, she sank a German submarine, she sank an auxiliary cruiser; and finally she herself was numbered among those that did not come back. The submarines that were engaged in mine-laying also had an occasional successful fight with enemy ships. Thus *E34*, while returning from a mine-laying expedition, made a clever attack on an enemy submarine. The two ships were on the surface, coming towards each other. The British submarine was the first to sight the other. She dived and fired a torpedo, which struck the German in the conning-tower. A violent explosion followed, and afterwards there was nothing to be seen on the water save two objects, one of which proved to be the German captain, who was saved, and the other to be one of the crew, who sank.

It is the practice of the submarine to deliver its attack when below the surface. There are, however, exceptions to this rule, as when the attack is made on a dark night, when it would be impossible to distinguish one's target through a periscope. Thus *E52*, of the Harwich Flotilla, in November 1917, while co-operating with the Dover Patrol, sighted an enemy submarine at about one o'clock in the morning; she attacked the enemy on the surface, and fired two torpedoes, both of which struck. The German sank, and only one survivor was picked up.

And now and again it was bigger game that was brought down, as when *E8*, of the Harwich Flotilla, at the time detached for service in the Baltic, struck the German heavy cruiser *Prince Adalbert* with a torpedo at eight hundred yards range. The torpedo must have caused an explosion in the German's magazine, for she was blown to pieces, and the submarine had to dive to prevent the falling fragments from injuring her.

Ingenious methods were employed by our submarines to entrap the enemy's ships, and especially their submarines. The following plan, for example, was successfully carried out by the

Harwich submarines until the Germans by chance discovered the trick and thenceforth became more wary. The enticing of the Hun to his destruction was effected in this manner. A disreputable old fishing vessel was sent out to potter about the North Sea as if trawling for fish, thus inviting the attack of the enemy. But the rope that was trailing ostentatiously over her side was attached to no innocent trawl-beam, but to one of our submarines, which she used to tow astern of her at a depth of about sixty feet below the surface of the sea. The trawler was commanded by a naval officer, and had a crew composed partly of blue-jackets and partly of trawler sailors. These trawler fishermen, by the way, eager to avenge their murdered brethren, were at first too zealous, and had to be prevented from uncovering the concealed gun which the trawler carried, so soon as an enemy was sighted, thus giving away the game. The trawler used thus to wander about the sea towing a submarine for about a fortnight at a spell; but the submarine was relieved by another submarine, always under cover of the night, every three or four days. The trawler, when she left port and when she returned to it, went alone, the submarine joining her or leaving her outside in the night. There was thus little chance of the Hun receiving information of what was doing.

Whenever an enemy ship, attracted by the bait thus displayed for her benefit, made for the apparently defenceless trawler with the object of sinking her, the trawler, by means of the telephone wire which connected her with the submerged submarine, communicated to the latter the movements of the enemy. The submarine—which was enabled by a device to slip the tow-line from within—when the right moment arrived delivered her attack, and a torpedo, possibly backed up by a round or two from the trawler's now disclosed gun, finished the enemy off.

I have before me quite a long list—and it is not a complete one—of the enemy ships that were sunk in action by the Harwich Submarine Flotilla, including cruisers, torpedo-boats, armed merchantmen, and submarines, the latter being the most numerous. It is satisfactory to know that, heavy though were the losses of the flotilla, the losses that they inflicted on the enemy (in action alone, exclusive of the terrible effect of the mines which they laid) were considerably heavier. But the glory of the little flotilla lies not so much in the material losses which it caused to the enemy as in the four years' sleepless watch which it kept in the North Sea, in conjunction with the other units of our Fleet—the watch that closed the oceans to Germany while holding them open to ourselves and our Allies, the watch that kept the great German Navy lying paralysed in its harbours, until the day came when the battleships that had not fired a shot crawled across the North Sea to surrender themselves ignominiously to our admirals.

CHAPTER 10

German Crimes

I will conclude this section of the book with two stories of submarines which will serve well to contrast Hun methods of sea warfare with our own. The first story shows how those who manned the German warships (one cannot employ the term "sailors" when speaking of Germans) treated a British crew when it was at their mercy and could not defend itself. The second story shows how our sailors acted in similar circumstances.

In the summer of 1915 the submarine *E13* was detached from the Harwich Flotilla and sailed to the Baltic. She went aground off Saltholm, an island in the Sound, near Copenhagen. A German destroyer came up and opened fire on her while she thus lay helpless. The captain of the submarine gave the order that she should be abandoned. This was done. The Huns then opened a heavy fire with shrapnel and machine-guns on the British sailors in the water, killing many of them. Shortly none would have been left alive, and the *E13* would have been added to the list of the submarines that did not come back, their fate unknown, had it not been for the providential appearance on the scene of a ship belonging to a nation of real sailors, who have known the chivalry of the sea from the earliest days. A Danish gunboat came up and placed herself between the submarine and the German destroyer, thus compelling the latter to cease firing. The Danes picked up the survivors, who amounted to about one-half of the crew.

In a letter that appeared in the *Morning Post*, a correspondent gives some further particulars of this incident:

The Danish gunboat compelled the Huns to cease firing on the defenceless crew of this submarine, stranded in Danish territorial waters. Wanton murder was added to the grave infringement of Danish territorial rights. Both the Danish sailors and the gunners on the naval fort overlooking the scene were burning with indignation, and were joyfully awaiting the order to open fire on the German vessel, if the latter had not immediately obeyed the Danish signal to stop these inhuman and illegal proceedings. And the people of Copenhagen found it extremely difficult to suppress their natural anger when the funeral of the victims took place amidst scenes of heartfelt sympathy.

And now for the other story. One day in March 1915, while a section of the Harwich Submarine Flotilla was outside the harbour, engaged in the work of training men in the use of the torpedo, the *Firedrake*, one of the three tender destroyers to the flotilla, sighted an object on the Shipwash, a long, narrow shoal that lies about ten miles east of Harwich. The captain of the *Firedrake*, wishing to satisfy himself as to the nature of this object, steamed nearer to it and discovered that it was the conning-tower of a submarine, obviously of a German submarine, as none of our own submarines was in the vicinity. The German was aground on the shoal and at the mercy of the British. As the *Firedrake* approached her, the German crew were seen to be standing on her upper deck, which was awash, and holding up their hands. When the destroyer got still nearer, the Germans jumped into the water and were soon picked up by the destroyer's boats, which had been lowered for the purpose. It was thought that all the men had been brought on board the *Firedrake*, when a man was observed to hurry up to the submarine's deck from below. He shouted and waved his hands frantically, and then jumped overboard. He was picked up and brought off, but volunteered no information as to what he had been doing before he had left his ship. This was soon made clear, however, for several explosions now followed each other on the stranded submarine, and bits of bedding and other articles and volumes of brown smoke were seen to be pouring out of her conning-tower.

It was a dirty trick to play after a surrender. Had the explosions occurred a few minutes later, we should probably have lost some of our own men, as boats were about to put off to the submarine with a boarding party. If the case had been reversed, and the crew of a British stranded ship had done this thing, the Germans would undoubtedly have shot them, had there been any left to shoot; for probably shell and machine-gun fire would have been playing upon our men both before they had abandoned the ship and afterwards while they were in the water—as witness the *E13*. The German prisoners taken from the submarine, however, were treated by the British in a humane fashion.

And yet, as it turned out, the treacherous Hun had yet another and more dangerous trap arranged for us. Time having been allowed for any possible further explosions on the enemy boat, Torpedo-Lieutenant Paterson and two other officers went off to her, in order to ascertain her condition. They found that the examination could be more easily carried out at low water. So two hours later, when the tide had fallen, they again visited the ship. She proved to be a submarine mine-layer, the *U. C. 5*, full of mines. She had been badly holed by the explosions, and the water was surging about inside of her. The admiralty were very anxious to salvage her, for she was the first German submarine that had fallen into our hands, and she would afford us the opportunity of learning whatever secrets a German "U" boat might contain. But it was obvious that it would be impossible to tow her into harbour without proper salvage plant. As it turned out, the salving of her proved a long job, occupying twenty-seven days of anxious and arduous work. A salvage officer and divers were got from the port to do the preliminary work and get all ready before the arrival on the scene of Commodore Young, R. N. R., and the heavy salvage plant. The mines in the submarine, of course, presented a serious danger, and Lieutenant Paterson was told off as mine adviser to the salvage people. First, exercising due caution, he made a careful examination of the wreck, which resulted in the discovery of what appears to have been the other Hun trap. He found that two of the mines had been loosed and were projecting through the bottom of the mine-tubes. Had attempts been made to raise the submarine, the mines would have fallen out, and their explosion would probably have annihilated the submarine, the salvage ships, and those engaged in the salvage work.

Lieutenant Paterson reported what he had discovered, and ordered all salvage operations to be suspended until these mines had been made safe. That this had been a deliberately planned trap on the part of the Hun is indicated by the following incident. Lieutenant Paterson was told that one of the prisoners taken from the *U. C. 5*, who was at that time confined in the *Pandora* depot ship, had asked if he could see a British officer, as he had a statement to make. So Paterson went to see him. The man then said that he had been very well treated by his captors, and that in recognition of this he wished to warn the English against making any attempt to salve the submarine, as a trap had been laid to blow up those who should undertake this task.

Lieutenant Paterson now proceeded to deal with the mines in the submarine; he had with him an expert and daring naval diver—the former was awarded a D. S. C. and the latter a Conspicuous Gallantry Medal and a gratuity, in recognition of their services on this occasion. It was highly risky work, calling for much dexterity and ingenuity. It was found that the two projecting mines could not be drawn back into the tubes, so they were secured where they were with wire in such a way that they could not fall out; though, of course, there still remained the possibility of their being exploded by the ship's bumping on the sand. The upper mines were then rendered innocuous by the removal of the acid tubes from the horns and other precautions, but it was impossible to do this with the lower mines, so they remained active.

Then the salvage work commenced—a heavy business now, for the *U. C. 5* was daily sinking deeper into the quicksands of the Shipwash. The naval salvage plant at Harwich proved too light to move her. At last she was lashed to a lighter with 6½-inch wire, which was passed round her in four parts. As the tide rose the lighter lifted the wreck a little way, and then the wires broke, and back the submarine fell to the sea-bottom, at imminent risk of exploding the two projecting mines. Finally, Commodore Young, R. N. R., the salvage expert under whom the admiralty salvage department has been placed, succeeded, with his heavy salvage plant, in raising her. He employed 9-inch wire and a large lighter capable of lifting 500 tons. The wreck was secured to the lighter's side at low water. The lighter's near tanks were then emptied, and her outer tanks were filled with water, which thus acted as a counterweight. This time the U. C. 5 was raised and got off safely. She was towed into Harwich harbour and placed in the floating dock—a delicate operation, as the measurements were close, the dock being only just large enough to receive her, and the two live mines were still projecting from her. But happily no accident occurred. All the mines were removed. She was patched up and sent to the Thames, where, it will be remembered, she was exhibited to the public and aroused much interest.

It was no small part in the naval war in the North Sea that was played by the light cruisers and destroyers of the Harwich Force and the Harwich Submarine Flotilla. Their province it was to haunt the enemy's coasts for four years in all seasons and weathers, and harass the Hun in his own waters. It is a story of daring strategy, ingenious devices, constant stubborn attack, and as stubborn defence. The facts speak for themselves.

PART 3

The Harwich Auxiliary Patrol and Mine-Sweeping Force

CHAPTER 11

The Royal Naval Trawler Reserve

Having in previous chapters dealt with some of the gallant doings in the war of the Harwich Force of light cruisers and destroyers and the Harwich Submarine Flotilla, I will now turn to a third force which had Harwich as its base—the Harwich Auxiliary Patrol and Mine-sweeping Force, whose most valuable and most dangerous work it was throughout the war to clear the sea routes of the enemy's mines over a large and very vulnerable portion of the North Sea, and, incidentally, to attack and destroy the enemy's mine-laying submarines whenever possible, thus keeping open and comparatively safe the channels used by the Harwich Force and those frequented by our merchant shipping.

A few years before the war the admiralty had the foresight to found what may now be regarded as the nucleus of the vast mine-sweeping organisation that has been developed since 1914. When war broke out this nucleus contained a personnel of about a thousand officers and men, belonging to the Royal Naval Trawler Reserve, who used to undergo a short training each year in mine-sweeping, as it was then known; for great indeed has been the progress made since in this by no means simple science. These men were quite apart from the active service ratings of Fleet Sweeping Flotillas. It was realised how utterly inadequate was so small a force for the gigantic task that lay before it, so the admiralty at once took steps to place the R. N. T. R. on a war footing. Able officers were set to work to organise the undertaking, suitable vessels were acquired, crews were enrolled, and the force expanded rapidly until at last it included approximately 750 sweeping vessels, all manned from the Trawler Reserve, the total of which was 38,000 at the conclusion of the armistice. The magnitude of the work carried out may be gathered from the fact that during hostilities about 2000 square miles of sea were swept daily for mines in our home waters alone, while nearly 10,000 enemy mines were swept up and destroyed.

The Harwich Branch of this force—the one with which I am here dealing—from the outbreak of war has been commanded by two successive commanders under the rear-admiral of the base. Both these commanders have been promoted to captains for good service during the war, while one has received the D. S. O., and the other the D. S. O. and bar.

This auxiliary unit during the war was composed of something under one hundred mine-sweeping trawlers, patrol trawlers, and mine-net drifters, with a complement of about fifteen hundred men. In the year 1916 it became apparent that the mine-sweeping force was not strong enough to cope with the large number of enemy mines laid in the area. Consequently the patrol trawlers were converted into mine-sweeping trawlers.

The vessels employed in mine-sweeping on our coasts are of various types. I will not touch on the Fleet Sweepers, the twin-screw ships, the gunboats, and other craft, attached to the Fleet, whose duty it is to search the approaches to the Fleet bases in advance of the Fleet, but will confine myself to a description of the work performed by the hired paddle steamers, trawlers, drifters, and motor launches that constitute the auxiliary force at the Harwich base.

First to speak of those sturdy little craft, the steam trawlers— as fine sea-boats as you will find the world over. They are of various sizes, the largest being of about 350 tons displacement. Their weatherly qualities make them excellent mine-sweepers; the powerful winches with which in time of peace they used to hoist in their trawl-beams enable them to deal efficiently with a mine-sweeping wire. Their draught, of from fourteen to sixteen feet, is certainly somewhat against them in their war work, but gives them a good hold of the water; and as these boats are somewhat down by the stern, their propellers are so deep that they never race in the heaviest weather. A certain proportion of them carry wireless. At the beginning of the war each trawler was armed with a three-pounder gun, which could pierce and sink a German submarine of the earlier type. Now the trawlers and drifters carry six-pounders, and in some instances twelve-pounders.

The writer was wont to go out to the Dogger Bank with the Hull trawlers long ago, when these were all sailing craft, well-found ketches, no steam being used save for the donkey engine, whose function it was to haul in the trawl-beam; the crew of each vessel consisting of five hands, including the small boy and the child cook. To him, as to all those who knew our North Sea trawlers in the pre-war days, the change that has been effected in the personnel of these vessels by war conditions is amazing. Yet these are the same men, the same rough, hard-bitten fishermen, as fine sailors as use the seas. As I knew them, many of the trawler skippers could not read or write, but they knew their North Sea. Charts they despised; with compass and lead alone they found their way unerringly even to the coasts of Iceland; for they carried a mental chart in their memories, and had an intimate knowledge of the soundings of all these waters. They could smell their way across the North Sea in the thickest weather, so to speak.

These men, who have been fishermen from infancy and have faced danger throughout their lives, brought up in the rough-est of schools, now belong to the R. N. T. R., the Royal Naval Trawler Reserve, and man the mine-sweeping trawlers. Some of them might appear rude in speech and manners to residents of garden cities, but to those who know them these are true men led by "captains courageous," and they call for the admira-tion and respect of all Englishmen for the way in which they have carried out their perilous duties throughout the war. The mine-sweeping trawler carries a crew of about fifteen men. One scarcely recognises in them the whilom fishermen. The skip-per of a craft that used to form part of a fishing fleet now has warrant rank and is smart in naval uniform. The men, too, wear the badges of a distinguished service. The discipline enforced in a mine-sweeping trawler now comes nearly up to the standard of the Grand Fleet ships. Skippers and men mostly come from the fishing ports of the North Sea—Hull, Yarmouth, and the others; Harwich itself, of course, is not a fishing centre. The mine-sweeping trawlers are organised in divisions of from four to seven vessels, each division being under the command of an R. N. R. lieutenant.

What I have said of the trawler skippers and crews also applies to those who man the North Sea drifters, which were taken from the fishing grounds to do their work among the minefields. These drifters are for the most part manned by hardy Scotch fishermen, who, like the East Coast trawler men, took to their new work as a duck takes to water. These drifters are of lighter draught than the trawlers, and so can be employed in shallower waters. They proved of great service, not only in mine-sweeping, but also for laying mine nets and for carrying out exploratory sweeps. They also took part in the hydrophone patrols, when several of these craft used to drift noiselessly, listening by means of their hydrophones for the sound of enemy submarines travelling below the surface. When a submarine was heard to approach, working in combination, they used to ascertain its position by taking cross bearings of the directions of the sound as given by their respective hydrophones, and gradually closed in on it. When the position of the submarine was definitely located, an attendant vessel was signalled to, which did its best to drop depth charges on the submarine, or, if it came to the surface, attacked it with gunfire. But it was, of course, possible for the enemy, who also carried his hydrophones, to slip away; and to successfully trap him by the above device was an event of rare occurrence. Like the trawlers, the drifters carry guns and depth charges.

The trawlers and drifters manned by the men who used to fish with these vessels before the war compose the greater portion of the Harwich auxiliary force. Shortly after the opening of the war the admiralty took over a number of ordinary paddle passenger steamers for the purpose of mine-sweeping, of which several belong to the Harwich mine-sweeping unit. These are commanded by R. N. R. captains; carry six-pounder or twelve-pounder guns, and depth charges. Being of relatively high speed—some of them attaining a sweeping speed of ten knots—they can cover a good deal of ground, and being of shallow draught they are well adapted for mine-sweeping in the Harwich area. For the tidal range in this portion of the North Sea is about eleven feet; consequently the paddle steamer, drawing considerably less than eleven feet, is enabled at high water to engage in sweeping without incurring much risk of striking a German mine, provided that the area has been searched at low water and no mines are visible on the surface. These paddle steamers, which in time of peace had carried thousands of pleasure-seekers on summer holidays, at once proved very successful in the work of war. In the year 1917 alone they destroyed approximately four hundred enemy mines in the immediate approaches to Harwich. On several occasions the vessels of this section had narrow escapes; one was twice mined, and one sank in fifty seconds after striking a mine.

And lastly we come to that interesting class in this heterogeneous force—the motor launches—the compact M. L. boats and other power boats of various types, most of which were privately owned pleasure craft before the war. Handy, rapid, of light draught, these have proved of great service, especially in enclosed and shallow waters. They are employed for patrol work, also for mine-sweeping, but are not powerful enough for this latter work, except under certain conditions. The duty for which they are very well adapted is the exploration of enemy minefields at low water, and the sinking of such moored mines as appear above the surface, as is not infrequently the case in consequence of the inaccurate laying of the mines. The German mines, I may mention, were mostly laid at eight feet below the sea-level at low water.

The motor launches are commanded by R. N.V. R. officers, for the most part yachting men, among them being barristers, solicitors, stockbrokers, and other professional men. They have proved that our amateur sailors who used to handle their own craft in peace-time know their work, can quickly adapt themselves to war conditions, and are of the greatest service to their country in time of war. They were ever ready at the call of duty to push out into the North Sea when the weather conditions were such as would have prevented any sane man from venturing forth in time of peace with craft so small. Like the gentlemen adventurers of old, they were out for high adventure, and they found it.

The mine-sweeping on the enemy minefields was, of course, the principal function of the Harwich auxiliary base. The mined areas that had to be dealt with by this force extended from the south of Lowestoft to the Naze and twenty miles to seawards, while the mine-sweepers of the force were also employed in advance of the Harwich Force on the mined areas on the further side of the North Sea. The Huns had diligently laid their mines in extraordinary numbers in the Harwich area. The German mine-laying submarines did their utmost to block the approaches to Harwich. Captured German mine charts testify to the magnitude of their operations. The Harwich auxiliary force had, therefore, to keep open a swept channel running along the coast, and also several other channels opening from this coast channel eastward, across the minefields, to the swept War-Channel beyond, which served as the highway for merchantmen and other vessels passing up and down the North Sea. It was also part of the duty of the Harwich boats to sweep the War-Channel so far as this channel passes along the Harwich area.

Throughout the war the mine-laying work of the Huns was continuous; that is, so fast as we cleared a channel of their mines, more were laid by their ever-busy submarines. Consequently the work of our mine-sweepers had also to be continuous. The Harwich mine-sweepers' duty was to sweep the above-mentioned channels each day. As light was needed to see and sink the mines after they had been cut adrift, the mine-sweepers used to begin their work at daylight, whatever the conditions of tide or weather, and until they had completed their task no shipping was permitted to proceed up the channels. The risk at low water to the mine-sweepers was therefore very great, and heavy were their losses. They could not await the comparative security of high water, and the preparatory exploratory work of the shallow-draught craft at low water could only be carried out when low water happened to occur at a very early hour, and even then the time available for exploration was very limited. Since the armistice, the mine-sweeping is conducted in far safer conditions. No unnecessary risks are taken; the preliminary exploration at low water can be done thoroughly, and the mine-sweepers can do their part at high water.

For an officer in charge of the War-Channel sweepers the responsibility was very great, and often he had to come to a quick decision when two or more possible courses of action were open to him and it was not easy to foresee which would be the right course, while to take the wrong one would probably mean horrible disaster. I will now give an example of such a situation. In the first place, let it be borne in mind that the conveyance by sea of our foodstuffs, munitions of war, and men was a matter of vital importance to England, and that delays in transportation had to be reduced to a minimum. The Germans, knowing this, for a long time directed all their mine-laying energy to that great highway of shipping, the swept War-Channel extending from the Sunk to the Shipwash light-vessels—the channel the daily sweeping of which was the charge of the Harwich mine-sweepers. Very often, owing to the tides being quite unsuitable for sweepers, the choice had to be made between two evils—stopping all traffic, or risking the sweepers and convoying the traffic through the danger zone.

Now, on the occasion to which I am referring the War-Channel sweepers commenced their work at daylight near the Sunk light-vessel, and sweeping northwards found themselves at 8 a.m., it being dead low water, in the middle of a dangerous freshly laid minefield about half way between the Sunk and the Shipwash lightships, and close to the line of buoys. As some of the mines were showing on the surface, and the others must necessarily have been close underneath, the order was given to stop all traffic. Unfortunately the traffic, and particularly the south-bound portion of it, was very heavy that day, and before all the vessels could be stopped and anchored many of them were in close proximity to the minefield. All, however, were safely anchored, and two hours later, when the flood tide was making, light-draught steamers were set to sweep the area. The job was a difficult one, for the sweepers had to twist and turn among the anchored vessels, and in two cases mines were swept up within fifty feet of these.

In these circumstances it became apparent that the area could not be properly cleared while the merchant vessels lay there at anchor, and some further action was necessary. The officer in charge was faced by a very difficult problem—either he had to keep the whole fleet held up indefinitely, or take the risk of losing one or two of them. In the words of one who told me this story, "If the officer in charge delayed the traffic the powers that be would damn him, and if he lost any of the ships he would be twice damned." So the officer in charge relied upon his lucky star to preserve him from both calamities. Choosing the most favourable time of tide, he ordered all vessels to weigh anchor and steam out of the minefield on a course at right angles to it. Happily all the ships got under weigh safely; the sweepers carried on and swept up eight mines on the ground where the merchantmen had been anchored, thus proving how dangerous had been the situation; and very soon after there were sixty-five vessels in sight steaming north and south along the line of buoys that mark the channel. As my informant said to me, "If anyone spoke of this incident to the officer who gave the order, he would probably shrug his shoulders and say, 'I was lucky'; but he, and he alone, knows what that dreadful hour of anxiety meant to him."

Despite all precautions, many merchant vessels were mined in the War-Channel in the course of the war; but these disasters were largely due to the carelessness of shipmasters, who at times neglected to comply with the instructions that had been given to them. How well the Harwich auxiliary vessels carried out their work, and how heavy that work was, the following figures show. In the year 1917, the total number of enemy mines swept up and destroyed by the mine-sweepers of the thirty-three bases of the British Isles amounted to 3400, of which over 1000 stand to the credit of the Harwich base. It is a notable fact, too, that in the same year 500 mines were destroyed consecutively in this area without the loss of a single merchantman, whereas the average for the United Kingdom had been one merchantman lost to thirteen mines destroyed.

CHAPTER 12

Work of the Auxiliaries

Without going into technical details, I will now give a brief explanation of the usual methods employed by the mine-sweeping trawlers of the Harwich base. Two trawlers steaming abreast at about four hundred yards distance apart tow a sweep wire eight hundred yards in length, an end of which is attached to each trawler. The wire thus drags astern in a great loop, which is kept at the requisite depth—that is, at a depth well exceeding the draught of the deepest ship which would travel across that area—by kites. This sweep wire is serrated, so that when towing it quickly saws through the moorings of the mines, which are thus released and rise to the surface. When two or more pairs of trawlers are sweeping in unison they adopt what may be termed an echelon formation. The second pair of mine-sweepers follows the first pair, at a safe distance astern, on a parallel course, but on an alignment that causes the space swept by the following pair of vessels to somewhat overlap that swept by the leading pair, so that no unswept space is left between the two. If a third pair of vessels follows, it takes up a similar position astern of the second pair; and so on, if there be other pairs engaged in the sweep. When a strong cross tide is running, to carry out this operation accurately is no easy task. But the skilled North Sea fishermen who man the trawlers are the right men for this sort of work. They rapidly acquire all the tricks of sweeping, and soon learn to detect a mine that has been caught in the sweep by the singing of the sweep wire, the feel of it, and other delicate signs. The mine-sweeping trawlers are accompanied by a vessel whose duty it is to sink or explode by rifle fire the released mines as they appear on the surface.

The above explanation of mine-sweeping, of course, deals with very elementary matter. For during the war this science has made immense progress, and volumes could be written on it. Many are the ingenious contrivances that have been introduced to improve the efficiency of the sweep. In fact, in all our operations, offensive and defensive, below the surface of the sea weird new inventions play an important part. Take, for example, that grimly humorous invention the indicator net, to lay which was one of the duties of the drifters of the Harwich Force. In its early form this was a fine wire net, which, when run into by a submarine travelling below the surface, was dragged from its moorings and remained attached to the enemy, accompanying him whithersoever he went, not impeding his progress, and possibly unnoticed by him, but dooming him to destruction. For attached to this net by a long line was a buoy containing a torch which was lighted automatically when the strain of the tow came on the buoy. So the unconscious enemy travelled on underneath, announcing his presence by the flaming torch which accompanied him overhead, thus enabling the watchful British patrol boats to close in on him and effect his destruction with depth charges. The above is an ideal case, for in practice the operation was by no means always so simple or so successful. But that early type of indicator net has been superseded by a much more deadly invention.

A great deal of useful work was done by the Harwich drifters in evolving the best method of working the indicator net, and their system was eventually adopted as standard by the admiralty. Great perfection was attained in this work. Thus, on one occasion in 1917 some Harwich drifters sailed to a certain destination in the North Sea, and after a week's work in laying and watching their nets destroyed three "U" boats. The crews received a reward of £3000 from the admiralty; for £1000 was the prize given for the total destruction of one of these enemy submarines.

The mine-sweeping has been described by those who should know as having been the hardest service in the North Sea during the war. Sir Edward Carson, who inspected the Harwich auxiliary force, in the course of a speech, likened the men employed in the mine-sweeping craft to soldiers in trenches at the front, who were required to go over the top every day. It was indeed arduous and hazardous work. The least of the dangers faced was that from the enemy Zeppelins and aeroplanes which were constantly bombing the vessels—but here, as elsewhere, with little effect; our fishermen took small notice of these overhead foes.

It is indeed remarkable how very little damage was ever done by Zeppelins at sea. On one occasion, it is true, the Zeppelin crews killed a number of their own countrymen—the survivors of the sinking *Blücher*—mistaking them for Englishmen. But our ships suffered practically nothing from their frequent attacks. Yet the enemy aircraft did their utmost to interfere with the operations of our mine-sweepers and mine-net laying drifters. On one occasion a Zeppelin hovered over a fleet of the latter craft which were lying in wait watching their deadly nets off the Shipwash. The Zeppelin dropped about seventeen bombs, some of which fell very close to the vessels, exploding violently and throwing up huge columns of water; but not a single hit was made and no damage was done.

But the mines amid which their duties took them daily were a very real peril. Out of the little Harwich force, twenty-two mine-sweepers were sunk by mines in the course of the war, while many others were mined—some more than once—but were brought safely back to port. The loss of life was heavy. Nearly one-quarter of the officers and men were killed in the course of the war. In the case of the trawlers there was small chance for the men when their vessel was mined under them; but these tough fishermen, whose trade had taught them to face danger from their childhood, carried on cheerily among the minefields through all the years of the war. Many heroic deeds stand to their account.

In times of peace, not few are the wrecks and gallant savings of life on the stormy North Sea. But in war-time, with the far graver peril from enemy mines and ships added to that of storm or thick weather, many were the disasters and many were the courageous rescues of crews and passengers by our mine-sweepers. In the period extending from the date of the establishment of the Harwich base up to December 31, 1917, no fewer than 1065 men, women, and children were picked up and saved from mined vessels by the Harwich mine-sweepers—a total which was much exceeded later. Often these craft hurried to the rescue at fearful risk of being struck themselves by mines of the same group that had brought about the disaster. One hears of trawlers that put out their dinghies in the roughest weather in order to save lives; for example, as when a trawler's dinghy rescued airmen from off the dangerous shoal of the Longsand when a heavy sea was breaking over it. For the North Sea fisherman, like his brethren in the navy, is imbued with that chivalry of the sea which makes the British sailor what he is.

And not only lives but ships with valuable cargoes of food were often saved. For example, there is the notable incident of the saving of the *Berwen*. In the rapidly falling darkness of a winter day, with a strong south-west gale blowing and a heavy sea running, the little wooden drifter *Lloyd George*, manned by ten hardy Scotch fishermen, while patrolling the War-Channel between the Shipwash and the Sunk light-vessels, sighted the large merchant steamer *Berwen*, apparently mined and not under control, to the south-westward of the Shipwash.

The *Lloyd George* immediately steamed at full speed to the assistance of the *Berwen*, only to find that the mined ship had been abandoned by her crew and was rapidly drifting on to a minefield which stretched to leeward of her, where several moored mines could be plainly seen at intervals in the rise and fall of the heavy sea. The skipper of the drifter, realising the danger and the necessity for immediate action, with great skill and wonderful seamanship placed his drifter alongside the *Berwen* and, having put three members of his crew of ten on board her, passed a tow-line and commenced to tow her to the south-west, away from the minefields.

The little drifter, not fitted for towing, having none of the necessary appliances on board, and not having the power to deal with so heavy a tow, could make little, if any, progress in the teeth of the ever-increasing gale; but she held on to the *Benven* and fought bravely on throughout the dark night, surrounded by the unknown dangers of mines, and was able at the coming of daylight to hand her charge over safely to the tugs for which she had wirelessed.

The *Benven* eventually reached the Thames with only a few hundred tons damaged out of the seven thousand tons of sugar which formed her cargo. One is not surprised to hear that a grateful country omitted to pay any salvage to the seamen who, by their gallant action, had rescued so valuable a cargo, on the ground that the sugar was government property.

Worthy of note, too, is the good work done by the trawler *Resono*. On November 17, 1915, when off the Galloper light-vessel, she witnessed the blowing up by a mine of the merchant steamer *Ulrikon*. She took off all the crew of the lost ship, and no sooner had this rescue been effected than another steamer, the *Athomas*, struck a mine and was badly injured by the explosion. Her crew abandoned her and were picked up. The officer commanding the *Resono*, observing that the *Athomas* was not in immediate danger of sinking, decided to salvage her. The men composing her own crew refused to go on board of her again, though it was explained to them that they would have to go through the minefield in any case, and that they would be safer in a ship of large tonnage than in a trawler. Therefore the captain of the *Resono* called for volunteers from his own crew, put them on board the *Athomas* despite the heavy weather, towed her safely away, and handed her over to the Sheerness Patrol in sheltered waters. The *Resono*, after having accomplished much good work, eventually was blown up by a mine off the Sunk light-vessel on Christmas Day, 1915.

Another well-known trawler was the *Lord Roberts*. During her long career of patrol work in the Harwich area she went to the assistance of many mined ships and rescued a very large percentage of their crews. Unfortunately, she was mined and lost in October 1916, with a loss of one officer and eight men. The *Lord Roberts* had become a familiar and welcome sight to the merchant vessels using the channels off Harwich, and there was sorrow when she was lost. One Trinity House pilot, missing her from her usual patrol ground, wrote a letter to the authorities asking what had become of "our old friend, the *Lord Roberts*."

As I have shown, a large vessel with watertight compartments has a fair chance of surviving the effect of a mine. But with the small vessel it is otherwise, and on her the effect of the explosion of a German mine is indeed terrible. Thus the official message reporting the loss, March 31, 1917, of the drifter *Forward III.*, of 89 tons, read, "*Forward III.* mined. No survivors." As far as can be gathered from the circumstances, the drifter must have struck the mine with her keel dead amidships, and when the smoke cleared away there was nothing to be seen on the water beyond a few broken pieces of wood. A large section of her wooden keel came down on end, pierced the deck of the drifter *White Lilac*, and remained standing upright, looking, as it was put to me, like "a monument to the gallant men who had gone."

The loss of the trawler *Burnley* in November 1916 affords another example of the total disappearance of vessel and crew after the striking of a mine. The *Burnley* was in charge of a subdivision of trawlers carrying out a patrol in the vicinity of the Shipwash light-vessel. At the close of the day the senior officer in the *Burnley*, relying on the superior speed of his vessel to overtake the others, ordered the two trawlers under him to proceed to their anchorage in Hollesley Bay. What exactly happened after this will never be known, but it is surmised that the *Burnley* stopped to investigate something suspicious. The *Holdene*, the senior of the other two trawlers, reached the anchorage as night was setting in, and had just dropped her anchor when a flash was seen on the eastern horizon. This was followed by a dull, heavy explosion, which shook the *Holdene* from stem to stern. The anchor was immediately weighed and the *Holdene* steamed at full speed to the scene of the explosion; but, though she cruised about for two hours in the darkness, nothing was to be seen of the *Burnley* or her crew. On the following day a fresh group of mines was discovered in the vicinity, so it is probable that the *Burnley* had struck one of this group very soon after the mines had been laid by German submarines.

Among the losses of the Harwich mine-sweepers may be noted that of the paddle steamer *Queen of the North*, which was mined and sunk while engaged in mine-sweeping. Despite the gallant efforts of her consorts, one officer and nineteen men only were saved, seven officers and twenty-two men being lost. Mine-sweeping in the War-Channel, as I have explained, had to be carried out whatever the weather, and in winter the weather conditions often made the work extremely hazardous. For example, on one occasion a division had swept up eleven enemy mines. Before any of these mines could be sunk by rifle fire a blinding snowstorm swept over the sea, making it impossible for the vessels to distinguish either each other or the drifting mines. Nevertheless the R. N. R. officer who was in command of the division, by exercise of good judgment, extricated his vessels from the dangerous area, and twenty minutes later, when the weather cleared, he was enabled to destroy all the mines.

One of the many dangers that attend mine-sweeping is caused by the occasional failure of the sweep wire to cut a mine adrift. The mine and its sinker come up the sweep wire when the latter is hove in, at the great risk of causing an explosion under the vessel's stern. Thus, the paddle steamer *Mercury*, while sweeping off the Sunk, brought up three mines and their sinkers in this way. An explosion resulted, which blew her stern off. Fortunately, no lives were lost. She was towed into port and placed in dry dock for repairs. She was an unlucky ship, for on her very first trip after the repairs had been effected she struck another mine while sweeping close to the scene of her former accident. On this occasion her bows were blown away and two lives were lost. Again she was towed back to port and repaired, and she is now once more engaged in mine-sweeping.

There is also a serious danger of a mine fouling a vessel's anchor and coming up with it to explode under the vessel's bows, as is shown in the case of the drifter *Cape Colony*, whose crew experienced a miraculous escape from death. On the evening of January 7, 1917, in company of other drifters, the *Cape Colony* laid her mine nets under cover of the darkness. She was then told off with another drifter to anchor in the vicinity of the Shipwash to work the hydrophones during the night. At daylight on the following morning the signal was given to weigh anchor. The mate of the *Cape Colony*, leaning over the bow to see the cable come in, suddenly saw the horns of a mine, apparently foul of the anchor, on the edge of the water and within a foot of the stem. With great presence of mind he jumped to the capstan and stopped heaving in, but was unable to reverse and lower away. He immediately shouted a warning, ran aft, and jumped into the sea, followed by the rest of the crew. The last man had just got into the water when a heavy swell rolled along, lifted the drifter's bow, and exploded the mine, which blew half the drifter into matchwood. She pitched forward and quickly sank by the head. The crew were rapidly picked up by the boat from the other drifter, none the worse for their adventure.

Mines in their tens of thousands still lie about the North Sea to endanger shipping, and probably it will take a year to clear them. For sweeping up these mines the admiralty are giving the men a special rate of pay, and only those who volunteer are now employed. The danger incurred is practically negligible when compared with the risk that attended these operations in war-time.

Conclusion

Even those querulous and ignorant pessimists who, during the war, used to ask, "What is the navy doing?" must now know what the navy has done. Our navy kept open the sea routes of the world to ourselves and our allies, while wholly closing them to our enemies. Had our politicians permitted it, the blockade by our navy would have brought the war to an earlier conclusion. The Germans, driven from the surface of the sea, put their trust in their murderous submarine campaign. Finding that this failed altogether against our navy, they directed it against the merchant shipping of the world. That attempt too failed. Our navy gradually mastered the submarines, until at last, towards the close of the war, the crews of the German "U" boats refused to put to sea. There was no great decisive naval action, for the good reason that the High Sea Fleet would not fight it out with our Grand Fleet, but retired to the shelter of the German minefields whenever it was attacked. In vain inferior forces were sent to tempt the enemy out. The German raids on the East Coast had no military value, and apparently had frightfulness as their sole object. Their fast ships used to rush across the North Sea under cover of the fog, bombard our undefended watering-places for half an hour or so, then hurry home again. These raids reminded one of the mischievous urchin who rings a front-door bell and runs away. But though there was no great naval action, there was plenty of hard fighting at sea; many a bold enterprise was carried through and many a gallant deed was performed.

Of the great British Navy the Harwich Forces formed but a small part, but they were typical of the whole navy, and it was no small part that they took in far the most important theatre of the naval war—the North Sea. And now the Harwich Force of light cruisers and destroyers and the Submarine Flotilla, having carried through their great duty, are to be dispersed over the four quarters of the globe. Many have already sailed to the West Indies, to the Mediterranean, to the China seas, and elsewhere. The close bands of brothers who fought and died together through the great war are now to be broken up; and it requires little imagination to feel that they are loth thus to separate.

In these forces lives a spirit that recalls that of the military orders in the chivalrous days of the Crusades, when gallant knights were banded together to fight and sacrifice themselves for a great cause. To live for a while in these ships is to find oneself in a purer, breezier atmosphere—an atmosphere of simple loyalty, old-fashioned patriotism, devotion to the Service, and cheery good-fellowship. These young men—for in the little ships they are all young men, full of the joy of life, though veterans in war with great experiences—make one feel sorry for the people who, in the coming millennium that is being prepared by the politicians, will never have the chance of fighting for their country on land or sea.

Englishmen, and especially English naval officers, are not given to display of sentiment; but the members of the Harwich Force are justly proud of that Force, and regard themselves as indeed forming a band of brothers. Thus, after the signing of the armistice, at a dinner which was given by the captains of the destroyers of the Harwich Force to the great sailor who commanded that Force during the war, someone recited the stirring speech which Shakspeare puts into the mouth of Henry V. before Agincourt. These memorable words indeed well fitted the occasion:

This day is called—the feast of Crispian:
He that outlives this day, and comes safe home,
Will stand a tip-toe when this day is named,
And rouse him at the name of Crispian.

He that shall live this day, and see old age,
Will yearly on the vigil feast his friends
And say—to-morrow is Saint Crispian:
Then will he strip his sleeve and show his scars,
And say, these wounds I had on Crispin's day.
Old men forget; yet all shall be forgot,
But he'll remember, with advantages,
What feats he did that day:
Then shall our names,
Familiar in their mouths as household words,—
Harry the king, Bedford, and Exeter,
Warwick and Talbot, Salisbury and Gloster—
Be in their flowing cups freshly remembered:
This story shall the good man teach his son;
And Crispian Crispin shall ne'er go by,
From this day to the ending of the world,
But we in it shall be remembered:
We few, we happy few, we band of brothers;
For he to-day that sheds his blood with me,
Shall be my brother; be he ne'er so vile,
This day shall gentle his condition:
And gentlemen of England, now a-bed,
Shall think themselves accurs'd they were not here,
And hold their manhoods cheap, while any speaks,
That fought with us upon Saint Crispin's day.

LEONAUR

ALSO FROM LEONAUR
AVAILABLE IN SOFTCOVER OR HARDCOVER WITH DUST JACKET

THE FALL OF THE MOGHUL EMPIRE OF HINDUSTAN *by H. G. Keene*—By the beginning of the nineteenth century, as British and Indian armies under Lake and Wellesley dominated the scene, a little over half a century of conflict brought the Moghul Empire to its knees.

LADY SALE'S AFGHANISTAN *by Florentia Sale*—An Indomitable Victorian Lady's Account of the Retreat from Kabul During the First Afghan War.

THE CAMPAIGN OF MAGENTA AND SOLFERINO 1859 *by Harold Carmichael Wylly*—The Decisive Conflict for the Unification of Italy.

FRENCH'S CAVALRY CAMPAIGN *by J. G. Maydon*—A Special Correspondent's View of British Army Mounted Troops During the Boer War.

CAVALRY AT WATERLOO *by Sir Evelyn Wood*—British Mounted Troops During the Campaign of 1815.

THE SUBALTERN *by George Robert Gleig*—The Experiences of an Officer of the 85th Light Infantry During the Peninsular War.

NAPOLEON AT BAY, 1814 *by F. Loraine Petre*—The Campaigns to the Fall of the First Empire.

NAPOLEON AND THE CAMPAIGN OF 1806 *by Colonel Vachée*—The Napoleonic Method of Organisation and Command to the Battles of Jena & Auerstädt.

THE COMPLETE ADVENTURES IN THE CONNAUGHT RANGERS *by William Grattan*—The 88th Regiment during the Napoleonic Wars by a Serving Officer.

BUGLER AND OFFICER OF THE RIFLES *by William Green & Harry Smith*—With the 95th (Rifles) during the Peninsular & Waterloo Campaigns of the Napoleonic Wars.

NAPOLEONIC WAR STORIES *by Sir Arthur Quiller-Couch*—Tales of soldiers, spies, battles & sieges from the Peninsular & Waterloo campaings.

CAPTAIN OF THE 95TH (RIFLES) *by Jonathan Leach*—An officer of Wellington's sharpshooters during the Peninsular, South of France and Waterloo campaigns of the Napoleonic wars.

RIFLEMAN COSTELLO *by Edward Costello*—The adventures of a soldier of the 95th (Rifles) in the Peninsular & Waterloo Campaigns of the Napoleonic wars.

ALSO FROM LEONAUR

AVAILABLE IN SOFTCOVER OR HARDCOVER WITH DUST JACKET

ZULU:1879 *by D.C.F. Moodie & the Leonaur Editors*—The Anglo-Zulu War of 1879 from contemporary sources: First Hand Accounts, Interviews, Dispatches, Official Documents & Newspaper Reports.

THE RED DRAGOON *by W.J. Adams*—With the 7th Dragoon Guards in the Cape of Good Hope against the Boers & the Kaffir tribes during the 'war of the axe' 1843-48'.

THE RECOLLECTIONS OF SKINNER OF SKINNER'S HORSE *by James Skinner*—James Skinner and his 'Yellow Boys' Irregular cavalry in the wars of India between the British, Mahratta, Rajput, Mogul, Sikh & Pindarree Forces.

A CAVALRY OFFICER DURING THE SEPOY REVOLT *by A. R. D. Mackenzie*—Experiences with the 3rd Bengal Light Cavalry, the Guides and Sikh Irregular Cavalry from the outbreak to Delhi and Lucknow.

A NORFOLK SOLDIER IN THE FIRST SIKH WAR *by J W Baldwin*—Experiences of a private of H.M. 9th Regiment of Foot in the battles for the Punjab, India 1845-6.

TOMMY ATKINS' WAR STORIES: 14 FIRST HAND ACCOUNTS—Fourteen first hand accounts from the ranks of the British Army during Queen Victoria's Empire.

THE WATERLOO LETTERS *by H. T. Siborne*—Accounts of the Battle by British Officers for its Foremost Historian.

NEY: GENERAL OF CAVALRY VOLUME 1—1769-1799 *by Antoine Bulos*—The Early Career of a Marshal of the First Empire.

NEY: MARSHAL OF FRANCE VOLUME 2—1799-1805 *by Antoine Bulos*—The Early Career of a Marshal of the First Empire.

AIDE-DE-CAMP TO NAPOLEON *by Philippe-Paul de Ségur*—For anyone interested in the Napoleonic Wars this book, written by one who was intimate with the strategies and machinations of the Emperor, will be essential reading.

TWILIGHT OF EMPIRE *by Sir Thomas Ussher & Sir George Cockburn*—Two accounts of Napoleon's Journeys in Exile to Elba and St. Helena: Narrative of Events by Sir Thomas Ussher & Napoleon's Last Voyage: Extract of a diary by Sir George Cockburn.

PRIVATE WHEELER *by William Wheeler*—The letters of a soldier of the 51st Light Infantry during the Peninsular War & at Waterloo.

LEONAUR

ALSO FROM LEONAUR
AVAILABLE IN SOFTCOVER OR HARDCOVER WITH DUST JACKET

ADVENTURES OF A YOUNG RIFLEMAN *by Johann Christian Maempel*—The Experiences of a Saxon in the French & British Armies During the Napoleonic Wars.

THE HUSSAR *by Norbert Landsheit & G. R. Gleig*—A German Cavalryman in British Service Throughout the Napoleonic Wars.

RECOLLECTIONS OF THE PENINSULA *by Moyle Sherer*—An Officer of the 34th Regiment of Foot—'The Cumberland Gentlemen'—on Campaign Against Napoleon's French Army in Spain.

MARINE OF REVOLUTION & CONSULATE *by Moreau de Jonnès*—The Recollections of a French Soldier of the Revolutionary Wars 1791-1804.

GENTLEMEN IN RED *by John Dobbs & Robert Knowles*—Two Accounts of British Infantry Officers During the Peninsular War Recollections of an Old 52nd Man by John Dobbs An Officer of Fusiliers by Robert Knowles.

CORPORAL BROWN'S CAMPAIGNS IN THE LOW COUNTRIES *by Robert Brown*—Recollections of a Coldstream Guard in the Early Campaigns Against Revolutionary France 1793-1795.

THE 7TH (QUEENS OWN) HUSSARS: Volume 2—1793-1815 *by C. R. B. Barrett*—During the Campaigns in the Low Countries & the Peninsula and Waterloo Campaigns of the Napoleonic Wars. Volume 2: 1793-1815.

THE MARENGO CAMPAIGN 1800 *by Herbert H. Sargent*—The Victory that Completed the Austrian Defeat in Italy.

DONALDSON OF THE 94TH—SCOTS BRIGADE *by Joseph Donaldson*—The Recollections of a Soldier During the Peninsula & South of France Campaigns of the Napoleonic Wars.

A CONSCRIPT FOR EMPIRE *by Philippe as told to Johann Christian Maempel*—The Experiences of a Young German Conscript During the Napoleonic Wars.

JOURNAL OF THE CAMPAIGN OF 1815 *by Alexander Cavalié Mercer*—The Experiences of an Officer of the Royal Horse Artillery During the Waterloo Campaign.

NAPOLEON'S CAMPAIGNS IN POLAND 1806-7 *by Robert Wilson*—The campaign in Poland from the Russian side of the conflict.

LEONAUR

ALSO FROM LEONAUR
AVAILABLE IN SOFTCOVER OR HARDCOVER WITH DUST JACKET

OMPTEDA OF THE KING'S GERMAN LEGION *by Christian von Ompteda*—A Hanoverian Officer on Campaign Against Napoleon.

LIEUTENANT SIMMONS OF THE 95TH (RIFLES) *by George Simmons*—Recollections of the Peninsula, South of France & Waterloo Campaigns of the Napoleonic Wars.

A HORSEMAN FOR THE EMPEROR *by Jean Baptiste Gazzola*—A Cavalryman of Napoleon's Army on Campaign Throughout the Napoleonic Wars.

SERGEANT LAWRENCE *by William Lawrence*—With the 40th Regt. of Foot in South America, the Peninsular War & at Waterloo.

CAMPAIGNS WITH THE FIELD TRAIN *by Richard D. Henegan*—Experiences of a British Officer During the Peninsula and Waterloo Campaigns of the Napoleonic Wars.

CAVALRY SURGEON *by S. D. Broughton*—On Campaign Against Napoleon in the Peninsula & South of France During the Napoleonic Wars 1812-1814.

MEN OF THE RIFLES *by Thomas Knight, Henry Curling & Jonathan Leach*—The Reminiscences of Thomas Knight of the 95th (Rifles) by Thomas Knight, Henry Curling's Anecdotes by Henry Curling & The Field Services of the Rifle Brigade from its Formation to Waterloo by Jonathan Leach.

THE ULM CAMPAIGN 1805 *by F. N. Maude*—Napoleon and the Defeat of the Austrian Army During the 'War of the Third Coalition'.

SOLDIERING WITH THE 'DIVISION' *by Thomas Garrety*—The Military Experiences of an Infantryman of the 43rd Regiment During the Napoleonic Wars.

SERGEANT MORRIS OF THE 73RD FOOT *by Thomas Morris*—The Experiences of a British Infantryman During the Napoleonic Wars-Including Campaigns in Germany and at Waterloo.

A VOICE FROM WATERLOO *by Edward Cotton*—The Personal Experiences of a British Cavalryman Who Became a Battlefield Guide and Authority on the Campaign of 1815.

NAPOLEON AND HIS MARSHALS *by J. T. Headley*—The Men of the First Empire.

LEONAUR

ALSO FROM LEONAUR
AVAILABLE IN SOFTCOVER OR HARDCOVER WITH DUST JACKET

CAPTAIN COIGNET *by Jean-Roch Coignet*—A Soldier of Napoleon's Imperial Guard from the Italian Campaign to Russia and Waterloo.

HUSSAR ROCCA *by Albert Jean Michel de Rocca*—A French cavalry officer's experiences of the Napoleonic Wars and his views on the Peninsular Campaigns against the Spanish, British And Guerilla Armies.

MARINES TO 95TH (RIFLES) *by Thomas Fernyhough*—The military experiences of Robert Fernyhough during the Napoleonic Wars.

LIGHT BOB *by Robert Blakeney*—The experiences of a young officer in H.M 28th & 36th regiments of the British Infantry during the Peninsular Campaign of the Napoleonic Wars 1804 - 1814.

WITH WELLINGTON'S LIGHT CAVALRY *by William Tomkinson*—The Experiences of an officer of the 16th Light Dragoons in the Peninsular and Waterloo campaigns of the Napoleonic Wars.

SERGEANT BOURGOGNE *by Adrien Bourgogne*—With Napoleon's Imperial Guard in the Russian Campaign and on the Retreat from Moscow 1812 - 13.

SURTEES OF THE 95TH (RIFLES) *by William Surtees*—A Soldier of the 95th (Rifles) in the Peninsular campaign of the Napoleonic Wars.

SWORDS OF HONOUR *by Henry Newbolt & Stanley L. Wood*—The Careers of Six Outstanding Officers from the Napoleonic Wars, the Wars for India and the American Civil War.

ENSIGN BELL IN THE PENINSULAR WAR *by George Bell*—The Experiences of a young British Soldier of the 34th Regiment 'The Cumberland Gentlemen' in the Napoleonic wars.

HUSSAR IN WINTER *by Alexander Gordon*—A British Cavalry Officer during the retreat to Corunna in the Peninsular campaign of the Napoleonic Wars.

THE COMPLEAT RIFLEMAN HARRIS *by Benjamin Harris as told to and transcribed by Captain Henry Curling, 52nd Regt. of Foot*—The adventures of a soldier of the 95th (Rifles) during the Peninsular Campaign of the Napoleonic Wars.

THE ADVENTURES OF A LIGHT DRAGOON *by George Farmer & G.R. Gleig*—A cavalryman during the Peninsular & Waterloo Campaigns, in captivity & at the siege of Bhurtpore, India.

ALSO FROM LEONAUR

AVAILABLE IN SOFTCOVER OR HARDCOVER WITH DUST JACKET

THE RELUCTANT REBEL *by William G. Stevenson*—A young Kentuckian's experiences in the Confederate Infantry & Cavalry during the American Civil War..

BOOTS AND SADDLES *by Elizabeth B. Custer*—The experiences of General Custer's Wife on the Western Plains.

FANNIE BEERS' CIVIL WAR *by Fannie A. Beers*—A Confederate Lady's Experiences of Nursing During the Campaigns & Battles of the American Civil War.

LADY SALE'S AFGHANISTAN *by Florentia Sale*—An Indomitable Victorian Lady's Account of the Retreat from Kabul During the First Afghan War.

THE TWO WARS OF MRS DUBERLY *by Frances Isabella Duberly*—An Intrepid Victorian Lady's Experience of the Crimea and Indian Mutiny.

THE REBELLIOUS DUCHESS *by Paul F. S. Dermoncourt*—The Adventures of the Duchess of Berri and Her Attempt to Overthrow French Monarchy.

LADIES OF WATERLOO *by Charlotte A. Eaton, Magdalene de Lancey & Juana Smith*—The Experiences of Three Women During the Campaign of 1815: Waterloo Days by Charlotte A. Eaton, A Week at Waterloo by Magdalene de Lancey & Juana's Story by Juana Smith.

TWO YEARS BEFORE THE MAST *by Richard Henry Dana. Jr.*—The account of one young man's experiences serving on board a sailing brig—the Penelope—bound for California, between the years 1834-36.

A SAILOR OF KING GEORGE *by Frederick Hoffman*—From Midshipman to Captain—Recollections of War at Sea in the Napoleonic Age 1793-1815.

LORDS OF THE SEA *by A. T. Mahan*—Great Captains of the Royal Navy During the Age of Sail.

COGGESHALL'S VOYAGES: VOLUME 1 *by George Coggeshall*—The Recollections of an American Schooner Captain.

COGGESHALL'S VOYAGES: VOLUME 2 *by George Coggeshall*—The Recollections of an American Schooner Captain.

TWILIGHT OF EMPIRE *by Sir Thomas Ussher & Sir George Cockburn*—Two accounts of Napoleon's Journeys in Exile to Elba and St. Helena: Narrative of Events by Sir Thomas Ussher & Napoleon's Last Voyage: Extract of a diary by Sir George Cockburn.

LEONAUR

ALSO FROM LEONAUR
AVAILABLE IN SOFTCOVER OR HARDCOVER WITH DUST JACKET

IRON TIMES WITH THE GUARDS *by An O. E. (G. P. A. Fildes)*—The Experiences of an Officer of the Coldstream Guards on the Western Front During the First World War.

THE GREAT WAR IN THE MIDDLE EAST: 1 *by W. T. Massey*—The Desert Campaigns & How Jerusalem Was Won---two classic accounts in one volume.

THE GREAT WAR IN THE MIDDLE EAST: 2 *by W. T. Massey*—Allenby's Final Triumph.

SMITH-DORRIEN *by Horace Smith-Dorrien*—Isandlwhana to the Great War.

1914 *by Sir John French*—The Early Campaigns of the Great War by the British Commander.

GRENADIER *by E. R. M. Fryer*—The Recollections of an Officer of the Grenadier Guards throughout the Great War on the Western Front.

BATTLE, CAPTURE & ESCAPE *by George Pearson*—The Experiences of a Canadian Light Infantryman During the Great War.

DIGGERS AT WAR *by R. Hugh Knyvett & G. P. Cuttriss*—"Over There" With the Australians by R. Hugh Knyvett and Over the Top With the Third Australian Division by G. P. Cuttriss. Accounts of Australians During the Great War in the Middle East, at Gallipoli and on the Western Front.

HEAVY FIGHTING BEFORE US *by George Brenton Laurie*—The Letters of an Officer of the Royal Irish Rifles on the Western Front During the Great War.

THE CAMELIERS *by Oliver Hogue*—A Classic Account of the Australians of the Imperial Camel Corps During the First World War in the Middle East.

RED DUST *by Donald Black*—A Classic Account of Australian Light Horsemen in Palestine During the First World War.

THE LEAN, BROWN MEN *by Angus Buchanan*—Experiences in East Africa During the Great War with the 25th Royal Fusiliers—the Legion of Frontiersmen.

THE NIGERIAN REGIMENT IN EAST AFRICA *by W. D. Downes*—On Campaign During the Great War 1916-1918.

THE 'DIE-HARDS' IN SIBERIA *by John Ward*—With the Middlesex Regiment Against the Bolsheviks 1918-19.

www.ingramcontent.com/pod-product-compliance
Lightning Source LLC
Chambersburg PA
CBHW032018090426
42741CB00006B/646

9780857066282